P R A

Nobody Told Me

If it were up to me, I would have every young person in America read this book (and because it's about sex, they would read it!). Pam Stenzel speaks boldly and honestly about sexuality in a beautiful way unlike anyone I know. This book is written in a style and format perfect for students to read and be challenged.

Jim Burns, Ph.D.
President of HomeWord and Author of *10 Building Blocks for a Solid Family, The Purity Code* and *Teaching Your Children Healthy Sexuality*

Having known Pam for more than a decade, I can attest to the fact that there is hardly anyone on the planet with more experience reaching out to teens about the dangers of lust and the rewards of purity. In *Nobody Told Me*, she offers straight answers to tough questions that every young person struggles with on a daily basis. With her characteristic wit and straightforward wisdom, she offers young people an antidote to the poison offered to them in our sex-saturated culture. Pam doesn't merely draw upon the collective wisdom that she has gained from reading medical journals and sociological studies. She taps into the insights she has learned from innumerable tearful conversations and riveting emails from teens. Their words, as well as hers, will inspire and encourage the reader of this book to hope for God's best and settle for nothing less.

Jason Evert
Author of *If You Really Loved Me, Pure Love* and *Theology of the Body for Teens*

I have admired Pam Stenzel's ministry for many years. Her straightforward approach provides teens all the information they need to make healthy sexual choices. Through a combination of peer stories and answered questions, Pam and Melissa have built on that greatness. This book has a creative, inviting approach that will provide every teen with a sense of understanding and empowerment through Christ to make wise decisions. No home, school or church should be without this text. It will undoubtedly change lives.

Josh McDowell
Author of *Why True Love Waits*

Pam Stenzel is *the* voice to today's generation regarding sex. *Nobody Told Me* is filled with personal stories from students that echo the hurt of having sex outside of marriage—and also true stories of students who waited. Pam writes just as she speaks: engaging, intense, mesmerizing. She always captivates an audience, and students walk away in awe of what they've learned. Pam doesn't simply say, "Don't have sex"; she unpacks the consequences of crossing God's barriers and shows the beauty of waiting for God's perfect gift. Presented in a popular Facebook style, students will love the captivating design and readability. This isn't simply another book on sexual purity or consequences; it's *the* book. Why? Because after finishing it, no reader will be able to say, "I didn't know. Nobody told me." This is a must-read for students and for anyone who works with students.

Susie Shellenberger

Editor, *SUSIE* Magazine

I love Pam Stenzel! Having known and admired her and her ministry for years, it is my joy to recommend *Nobody Told Me* to you. With interactive stories from young people across the nation, this book is relevant, powerful and packed with truths that all young people need to hear. I was encouraged as I read this book, and you will be too.

Rebecca St. James

Bestselling Christian recording artist and author

nobody
told me

nobody
told me

What You Need to Know About the Physical and Emotional
Consequences of Sex Outside of Marriage

PAM STENZEL AND
MELISSA NESDAHL

Regal

From Gospel Light
Ventura, California, U.S.A.

Published by Regal
From Gospel Light
Ventura, California, U.S.A.
www.regalbooks.com
Printed in the U.S.A.

Library of Congress Cataloging-in-Publication Data
Stenzel, Pam, 1965-
Nobody told me : what you need to know about the physical and emotional consequences of
sex outside of marriage / Pam Stenzel, Melissa Nesdahl.
p. cm.
Includes bibliographical references (p.   ).
ISBN 978-0-8307-5653-7 (trade paper)
1. Chastity. 2. Christian teenagers—Religious life. 3. Sexual abstinence—Religious aspects—
Christianity. 4. Sex instruction for teenagers—Religious aspects—Christianity.
I. Nesdahl, Melissa. II. Title.
BV4647.C5S73 2010
241'.66—dc22
2010035102

Rights for publishing this book outside the U.S.A. or in non-English languages are
administered by Gospel Light Worldwide, an international not-for-profit ministry.
For additional information, please visit www.glww.org, email info@glww.org, or write
to Gospel Light Worldwide, 1957 Eastman Avenue, Ventura, CA 93003, U.S.A.

To order copies of this book and other Regal products in bulk quantities,
please contact us at 1-800-446-7735.

Dedication

*To all those who have poured out their hearts, shared their
joy and their pain, asked the hard questions and shared so much
hard-earned wisdom, I am eternally grateful.*

*To all the amazing women and men who give their
lives serving in the Pregnancy Care Centers around the world,
you are truly the hands and feet of Jesus. May you be blessed
beyond measure for your selfless love.*

*To my family, who have endured long absences and
have always kept my feet on the ground. Without your
support and understanding, these pages would not
have been written. Love you so much.*

Pam Stenzel

Contents

Introduction

What's the Big Deal?

Dear Reader,

You live in a culture bombarded with sexual images and messages. From the moment you rise in the morning to the time you hit the pillow at night, messages about relationships and sex are thrown in your face. If you innocently turn on the radio to get ready in the morning, you hear Lady Gaga spewing, "I want your ugly. I want your disease. I want your everything as long as it's free." Once you get to school, many of you sit through "safe sex" talks in health class and maybe even have school nurses that hand out condoms, promoting the lie that you can have physical relationships without consequences. Your magazine ads are pushing the boundaries of pornography, and sexually explicit television shows parade couples cheating, random hookups and teens trying to get pregnant, as though these actions are "normal" and won't harm your future. Nothing could be further from the truth.

With more than 30 years of combined experience, we have seen firsthand how today's lies have marred your generation. Approximately 23 years ago, Pam began counseling in pregnancy centers in the Minneapolis/St. Paul area. Sitting in the client room with young women and men facing unplanned pregnancies, hearing positive results from testing for a sexually transmitted disease (STD), and heartache from broken relationships, she heard time and time again, "I didn't know. If somebody had told me this would happen to me, I would have made a different choice." After nine years of listening and learning from clients, Pam decided to transform defeat into victory and began delivering her "Sex Has a Price Tag" message to an international audience.

Melissa vowed 11 years ago, after watching countless tears fall and hearing the same comments from pregnancy center clients in South Dakota, that she would educate teens about the importance of abstinence in order to side-step lifelong pain and enjoy enduring healthy relationships. That vow led Melissa to work with Pam, and as a team they have communicated with teens and created abstinence curriculum for the last eight years.

We know that your fast-paced world requires you to make choices every day that could change your tomorrow. Maybe you've picked up this book having made a commitment to God and your future spouse that you will remain pure until your wedding day. If that is the case, then good for you— but do not put this book down. What you read will offer a window into the heart of your peers, providing answers so that you can accurately help your friends with their questions, as well as strengthen and encourage you in your choice to abstain from sex until marriage. Or, perhaps you've had sex, and a voice inside of you is saying, "Put this book down. It's too late for you." Don't listen. Within these pages are stories of teens sharing their struggles right alongside yours, and laced within the message is clarity where there has been confusion, hope where there has been pain, and practical steps to a redeemed future.

Through a unique combination of our expertise and your questions and experiences, we bring you the truth about important topics related to sex and dating so that you don't have to be the next person standing before a physician, counselor, parent or future spouse with regret and say, "Nobody told me."

SECTION ONE:

The Truth and Lies About Our Sexuality

Chapter 1

God's Amazing Blueprint

 Pam: God wants you to have great sex.
Comment On This · Love This · Shares with Friends

 Meta: I saw your post and had to write. I'm 22 years old and have been married for three months now. I first heard you speak about seven years ago at the Kingdom Bound festival in western New York. At that festival, my best friend and I were very compelled by what you said. We prayed for our future spouses and for chastity. Your message about being a princess got me through four awkward years of high school. In college I learned the fullness of the Church's teaching on sex in marriage. I also met an amazing man there. With your encouragement, both my best friend and I held strong to our wedding days and we, as virgins, proudly wore white coming down the aisle to our virgin husbands.
Comment On This · Love This · Share with Friends

 Pam: *Congrats* to you and to your best friend! As children of the King, He wants the very best for us; and because you followed His design, you got the very best. God's blessing on you in your new marriage.
Comment On This · Love This · Share with Friends

📝 **Note: God's Design for Good Sex.** Years ago, when I began speaking to students about sexual purity, I would use a very "hands-on" example. I brought with me a thick piece of scrap wood, a large nail and a cheap plastic alarm clock. Then I would ask for a volunteer from the audience and ask him/her to come up onto the stage. I instructed him/her to pound the nail into the wooden board with the alarm clock. Obviously, when the volunteer tried to pound in the nail, the cheap clock broke into lots of plastic shards. The alarm clock was *not* intended to be able to drive a nail. It was *intended* to wake you up!

God created you and me in His image! God is the designer of our bodies and our souls! And as the designer, as the "clock maker," He has given us an instruction manual on how our bodies and souls should be used! If we decide to ignore the design, we are shaking our fist in the face of the designer, God Himself. When we refuse to read the instruction manual, there will be disastrous results. We may end up like that broken alarm clock, bits of plastic that are no longer whole and unable to be used for its intended purpose.

God didn't create just your body. He created your sexuality as well! The design is amazing! He created man first, and then, like a perfect matching puzzle piece, He created woman. Both are unique, but when joined together become "one flesh." You've heard the famous *Jerry Maguire* movie line, "You complete me." But did you know those words come straight from Genesis 2? After creating man, God saw that it was not good for him to be alone (see Genesis 2:18), and thus He created woman (from Adam's one rib) to be Adam's helpmate (see v. 21). Along with this beautiful creation, God blessed their *union* (sex) and designed it to accomplish an amazing task—procreation! Man and woman actually become "creators," with God Himself, of new life! Not only is this a miracle, but it is also an incredible privilege! Even more, God gave them instructions to "Be fruitful and multiply!" He *commanded* them to have sex! God is not "anti-sex" or prudish. Exactly the opposite, He is *pro-sex*!

Since it is God who created our sexuality and sex itself, He has the right to give us the instructions on how to use this incredible gift! And He made His instructions clear! Sex is to be between a man and a woman who have entered into a covenant of *exclusive, lifelong commitment*. God created sex to be expressed ONLY in this covenant commitment—not just with someone you happen to "feel loving" toward at any given moment. When we commit ourselves to following God's instructions, we will experience His blessing! When we ignore His instructions and use our sexuality for our own pleasure, without the covenant of marriage, we experience pain! This happens not because God is vindictive but because we ignored the instructions and used our sexuality for a purpose and to fulfill a desire for which it was never intended!

Gigi: Great post, Pam! Almost 10 years ago, I sat in the office of a new doctor and, as usual, the nurse drilled me with questions. "Do you use drugs?" "No." "Sex?" "Never." Stunned, the nurse replied, "What? You've never had sex? How old are you?" Feeling slightly annoyed, I answered, "Twenty-three." She looked at me like I had eight heads. "Don't you ever want to have sex?" she asked, to which I replied, "Well, of course! But with my future husband."

I have just finished three years as a parish youth minister. It is one of the hardest things I have ever done. The teens are faced with so many trials, but the thing that seems to get their attention the most is the subject of sex and their relationship with members of the opposite sex.

We see gangs, drugs, suicide, war, rape, abortion and a litany of other problems that our teens face today. What does it all mean, and how can we bring about change in such a sick, lust-saturated world where sex is degraded to the idea of looking at our fellow human beings as mere objects? How can we get to the point that we reflect upon the meaning, sacredness and value of the human body, and then embrace it and live it in our own lives? Think about it. Do you think if we valued our bodies, gangs would kill one another? Do you think if we valued our bodies, we would infest it with drugs? The list goes on and on.

Many Christians sadly grow up thinking of their bodies as obstacles to their spiritual life, when in reality, Christianity says the body is "so good you can't even fathom it."[1] It says how amazing, how sacred, what a glimpse of heaven not only are our bodies, but when a husband and wife make love, each time they are renewing their wedding vows. Many people may see the teachings of the Church as oppressive rules; however, the gospel is meant to change our hearts so that we no longer need the rules. To the degree that we experience this change of heart, we experience freedom from the law (see Romans 7 and Galatians 5). What a glorious, redeeming message of hope for all of us!

I turn 33 on April 15. I have lots of male and female friends that I laugh, cry and pray with. I hope one day to meet my earthly husband, who God designed just for me, and give and share with him two of my most precious gifts: my faith and my virginity. I hope he is out there; but whether that day comes or not, I know one thing to be certain— I am a bride of Christ, desired, loved and cherished for all eternity.

Comment On This · Love This · Share with Friends

Pam: Gigi, AWESOME! Thank you so much for sharing your heart and being a witness for Christ!

Comment On This · Love This · Share with Friends

Pam: I love the simplicity of God's love and His instructions about sex. This is not a complicated rule: If you are not married, don't do it. If you are married, go for it . . . with the person you are married to!

Comment On This · Love This · Shares with Friends

Logan: I don't understand what the difference is between being married and just being committed to each other. It seems that if you know that you are going to be with the person for the rest of your life, and you are committed to her, that should be enough! Isn't saying that sex can only be in marriage a little restrictive?

Comment On This · Love This · Share with Friends

Pam: Before I answer that question, I want you to think about the last "committed relationship" you were in. Or, if you have never been in a serious relationship, I am sure you have a friend or two who has. Now, if you wanted to END this relationship, how would you do it? Maybe you would have another friend tell the person that you do like them a lot but would prefer to "back off a little" and be friends? Maybe you would have the courage to attempt to sit down with her face to face and break up that way. I have to believe there are a few of you who might simply suggest texting the person or changing your Facebook status! Now, if I wanted to "break up" with my spouse, what would it take? A LOT MORE than a heart-to-heart conversation or a text message. It would take an attorney and half my stuff!

This question kind of reminds me of the question, "Can I worship God and be a good Christian but never go to church?" Typically, this is about laziness, a lack of real priority for your relationship with God and a general fear of "tying" yourself down to a community of believers who can encourage you and even hold you accountable for your behavior. It's like saying, "God, I want a relationship with You, but I don't really want to be *with* You or any of Your friends. Can we just keep this private?" Couples that begin to justify "behaving" as if they were married—having all the "perks" of an intimate sexual relationship with NONE of the responsibility—are really saying the same thing. They want the privileges that come with intimacy, but none of the work. Even worse, they are continually communicating a "lie" with their bodies! They are saying "we are one flesh" with their behavior without the covenant to back it up.

Marriage is a covenant, not a contract. A contract is a legally binding promise made by two persons for the exchange of "goods and services." A covenant is actually the exchange of *persons* and is always between persons and *God!* Marriage is considered one of the first and oldest sacraments of our faith—the covenant between God, and man and woman. It should never be entered into lightly. Marriage is also sacramental. David Hajduk, in his book *God's Plan for You*, explains:

> The grace that flows from Christ's giving of himself—freely, totally, faithfully and fruitfully in and through his body for the good of his Bride, the Church—enables Christian spouses to do the same through the sacrament of marriage. Because of this outpouring of grace, Jesus can command his followers to live out God's plan for marriage from the "beginning." They have become new men and women in Baptism, remade in the image of Jesus Christ, and therefore as spouses are to be the physical image of the Trinity and the physical representation of Christ's love for the Church in the world. And the sacrament of marriage makes all this possible. This sacrament is initiated by means of the spoken vows, or mutual consent, blessed and approved by God.[2]

Comment On This · Love This · Share with Friends

Christina: I was hoping you could help me with something. I was trying to explain to friends why premarital sex is unbiblical, but they still think that it's okay to have sex and do all the other stuff as long as you love the person and plan on marrying them. Can you direct me to any verses where it actually says "don't have sex until you're married"?

Comment On This · Love This · Share with Friends

Pam: The Old Testament law is very clear. *Adultery* is actually defined as *any form of sex outside of marriage*. You can't be "kind of married" or "almost married"; you either are or you are not. (Just like you can't be "kind of pregnant" or "half pregnant." You ARE or ARE NOT!)

The New Testament word is even clearer! The Greek word that most of the time is translated in English as "sexual immorality" is actually *pornea* (which is the root of the word "pornography"). *Pornea* not only includes an act of sex outside of marriage (fornication, adultery), but it also includes watching others have sex, pornography, exposing your genital area, and so on. It is a much broader definition. Again, either you are married and having sex with only that person, or you are not!

Most pastors tell couples in premarriage counseling that if they are currently having sex or have had sex prior to marriage, what they are actually saying to each other is that they are *perfectly comfortable* having sex with someone they are *not married to*! What will a ceremony change? NOTHING! You have already broken the commandment, seemingly without a conscience. You have NO sexual discipline! A beautiful white dress and nice black tux do not magically transform the core of your integrity.

Comment On This · Love This · Share with Friends

💕 Lisa's Story

As a young director of a new Pregnancy Care Center, I relied heavily on a local Christian college to provide me with interns. They were always full of life and came to the ministry with a lot of passion. Also, because they were college students, they were often much closer in age to the clients we were seeing and related to their struggles very well. This is how I met and came to know Lisa. In her senior year at a local Christian college, she loved the girls she counseled and poured her heart and soul into helping them. Lisa was engaged to marry a young man who was also a student at the university, and who was training to be a pastor. They had such a bright future planned, and both wanted to honor God with their lives and ministries.

Just after Christmas break, when Lisa returned to her internship at the center, I noticed a definite change in her demeanor. She seemed distant and was reluctant to do the pregnancy tests of girls coming to our center. She would try to give me an excuse, but I remembered that during the semester before this one she would have been disappointed if no one came in for counseling during her shift, and now she was doing everything to avoid clients! When I asked her if everything was okay, she simply brushed it off as stress with school and the upcoming wedding in June.

One late night in February, I received a horrible phone call. Lisa's roommate called me at home to tell me that Lisa had attempted to take her own life and was in the hospital. On my drive downtown to the hospital, I prayed for wisdom beyond my own. I didn't know what had happened to this godly young woman with such a bright future! After a few minutes by her bedside, the truth came out. Lisa and her fiancé had engaged in sex over the Christmas break while visiting his family. At first, they both justified their decision to have sex with thoughts that the wedding was only a few short months away. They were "almost" married! But both realized that this was just a human justification for what they knew to be sin. They were NOT married; they were engaged! Lisa pointed to her purity ring that she still wore on her left hand. She told me that every time she looked at it, she thought about the "covenant" with God she had broken and realized that if she could justify breaking that covenant, she would justify breaking others. Then the unthinkable happened. Her fiancé broke off the engagement. I am not sure of all his reasons to this day (I never spoke directly with him), but I wonder if the guilt he was feeling led to his inability to make a commitment to Lisa. She was devastated. Her life was over. Or so she thought.

Lisa recovered physically from her attempt on her life, but it was many months of counseling and spiritual help that brought about her "soul" recovery. Lisa came to understand the forgiveness of a God who knew her unfaithfulness and loved and accepted her anyway. She also committed to God to NEVER AGAIN break her commitment to purity before marriage and continued to wear her purity ring, without condemnation, but as a symbol of her new commitment.

Lisa's pain could have been avoided. Her commitment to purity could have saved her many months, if not years, of pain. Today she tells students in her ministry that you are *not married* until you are married! She helps them understand that even engagement promises with rings, and wedding invitations and dresses bought, can be broken. Even though God restored her life and redeemed her pain, how much better to have listened to His instruction *first* and avoided the pain altogether!

📰 **News Flash:** Sexual intimacy produces more broken relationships than strengthened ones. Dr. Robert Blood, in his book *Marriage*, cites that "in a major study, more engagements were broken by couples who had [premarital sex]" than with couples who abstained. "The more frequent the intercourse, the larger the proportion of rings returned."[3] God's law is not about ruining your fun or wrecking your weekend. It's designed to protect you.

Pam: God created sex with a boundary. Inside of that boundary it's awesome. Kind of like fire. When it's negative 40 degrees in Minnesota, fire heats my house and looks pretty. But if that fire was in the middle of my living room floor, it would not be so awesome. It could burn my house down or hurt my family. Keep sex where it belongs!

Comment On This · Love This · Shares with Friends

Brandon: I have not been in a situation yet where I've had to say yes or no to sex. Could you share some Scripture verses for me to memorize so that I have the strength to say no when the time comes?

Comment On This · Love This · Share with Friends

Pam: Great plan, Brandon! Being connected with God's Word and knowing what He has to say empowers us to make healthy choices. And He has a lot to say about purity. Here are some passages I would encourage you to commit to memory:

Flee from sexual immorality. All other sins a man commits are outside his body, but he who sins sexually sins against his own body. Do you not know that your body is a temple of the Holy Spirit, who is in you, whom you have received from God? You are not your own; you were bought at a price. Therefore honor God with your body (1 Corinthians 6:18-20).

The acts of the sinful nature are obvious: sexual immorality, impurity and debauchery (Galatians 5:19).

But among you there must not be even a hint of sexual immorality, or of any kind of impurity, or of greed, because these are improper for God's holy people (Ephesians 5:3).

Put to death, therefore, whatever belongs to your earthly nature: sexual immorality, impurity, lust, evil desires and greed, which is idolatry (Colossians 3:5).

It is God's will that you should be sanctified: that you should avoid sexual immorality; that each of you should learn to control his own body in a way that is holy and honorable (1 Thessalonians 4:3-4).

Marriage should be honored by all, and the marriage bed kept pure, for God will judge the adulterer and all the sexually immoral (Hebrews 13:4).

Comment On This · Love This · Share with Friends

Pam: I was just watching Rebecca St. James's video "Wait for Me" on YouTube and remembering the last time I saw Rebecca backstage at a music festival in Iowa. (You can find a link to Rebecca's song on the *Nobody Told Me* Facebook fan page.) While there, I got a chance to "reintroduce" her to my son. When he was just three months old, she sang a cute kangaroo lullaby and rocked him to sleep on a tour bus ride through Kansas. I have to admit, when I was initially asked to work with an 18-year-old up-and-coming Christian artist, I was apprehensive. Concerned that young fame would evoke a diva or prima donna mentality, I questioned the humble, living faith she would have, but I was completely blown away by Rebecca. She was so humble and kind, and she radiated the true love of Jesus in a way I never expected. At the age of 18, she was a mature woman of God! When she sings "Wait for Me," she means it. It is not an act. It is a real woman of God willing to wait for a real man of God and honoring her savior with her whole life!

Comment On This · Love This · Shares with Friends

Phil: I saw your link. And I loved the song, but how do I know the sex with my wife will be good if we never have sex before we get married?

Comment On This · Love This · Share with Friends

Pam: Let me remind you that if you choose to wait until marriage and you marry someone that has *only* been with you, there is no comparison. You will be each other's best! And, by standing strong yourself, you can be sure that your spouse is the only one on your mind that night. What an amazing gift! This isn't about competition or performance. This is about experiencing sexuality at its best!

Comment On This · Love This · Share with Friends

Jaci: Thank you for the encouragement. I am a 23-year-old girl who made a commitment to purity after watching one of your videos when I was 15. I have been faithful to that promise and covenant I made before God, family and friends 8 years ago. I have felt alone in this commitment to purity. I'm the only 23-year-old I know who has never been kissed, although I've had my share of crushes. But I believe God has hand-chosen one special man for me, and I've been praying for him since I made that commitment to purity. You are making a difference!

Comment On This · Love This · Share with Friends

Pam: Awesome!! Thanks for the amazing testimony. God will *honor* your faithfulness! And we give thanks for *His grace* that equips us to *live holy lives for Him!* This made my day. My suggestion to you and to all my friends would be to write a letter to your future spouse letting him/her know how you are choosing to honor them in your lives now so that you can put in words your promises, stick to them and gift your spouses on your wedding day with that note, letting them realize how you've cherished them for so long.

Comment On This · Love This · Share with Friends

💬 Melissa's "Note to My Future Spouse"

Dearest future husband,

Right now I am praying for you and I wanted you to know. You see, because I've made promises to God, I've already made promises to you.

Like most girls, I've dreamed of my wedding day since I was young. I can't wait to pick the beautiful flowers and designer cake. More fun yet will be shopping for the gorgeous white dress for the day we say, "I do."

But that dress will be more than just a white dress worn out of tradition. For you, that white dress will indicate the purity of my body and the physical restraint we have practiced to get to our special day. I love God with all my heart, and He made me for you. So I have waited for you. For this day. For this moment. And, I can't wait.

Since you are getting this letter, YOU are the one that waited with me. Thank you.

There are two things that I have been looking for in a spouse. One is to be a man who loves God. I love Him with all my heart, and in order for you to have my heart and parent my children, Christ must lead and inspire you. The other is to be a family man. I want to be a mom someday, and I will trust that you will be a strong husband and father if while we dated you treated your family well and enjoyed spending time with them. You are reading this, so you have fulfilled what I was looking for. I am blessed.

While I wait for you, I promise to continue praying for you—that God would help you stand strong. And I will keep my eyes on Him. I will date carefully. I will be honest about my faith and make verbal my promise to abstain until marriage. I will enjoy group dates and make sure that there is a plan during any one-on-one time. I will be strong because I love you.

I won't date just any guy, because my dad set the bar high. My mom and dad are like a couple that forgot their honeymoon ended. I see my dad smile when my mom walks in the room. I see him give her a kiss when she walks by. He adores her. And they worship together and share their faith with me. I want that, so I will only date a guy that cherishes me like my dad cherishes my mom.

With Christ in our life, and being careful to honor God now, I look forward to the marriage we will share. Oh, and Happy Wedding Day. Our day is here. We are Mr. and Mrs.!

Love, Melissa

Molly Kelly: How do we want our air? Pure. How do we want our water? Pure. How do we want sex on our wedding night? Pure. There is no greater gift a man and woman can give each other on their wedding night than the gift of their virginity. And it's a gift you can only give once.

Comment On This · Love This · Shares with Friends

 Pam: Molly! I LOVE it!

Comment On This · Love This · Share with Friends

 Pam: God did something at the beginning of time that, if I were Him, I would not have done, and that is why He is God, and I'm not. He took a colossal risk. He let us choose, knowing full well that we would all shake our fist in His face. What would follow would be sin, disease and death. We have to choose to follow Him. We have to choose to *obey* Him. We have to choose to return His love.

Comment On This · Love This · Shares with Friends

 Ashley: I'm worried about my friend Joy. She has this list of guys that she likes and wants to date. Her relationship with her parents isn't good, and she seems to think she will find happiness through a boyfriend. What do I say to her?

Comment On This · Love This · Share with Friends

 Pam: Thanks for caring about your friend and wanting to reach out to her! Unfortunately, the problem you are describing with Joy is all too common. It is human nature to fill a "void" in relationships with counterfeits. Sometimes girls who lose a parent, or whose parents are emotionally absent, will continually fill this void with sexual relationships, expecting "intimacy" but only getting emptiness. Sadly, it sometimes takes a lot of broken relationships before someone figures out that *no human person* can fill this need.

When Jesus confronted the Samaritan women at the well and asked for water, He said to her, "If you knew the gift of God and who it is that asks you for a drink, you would have asked him and he would have given you living water" (John 4:9). She asked Jesus to tell her about this water, and He told her to go get her husband, come back and He would tell them both (see John 4:16). She said, "I have no husband" (v. 17). Jesus replied, "You are right. . . . You've had five husbands, and the man you now have is not your husband" (vv. 17-18). Why did Jesus confront her this way? Was He being mean? I believe Jesus was looking deep in her soul and plainly asking, "Are you tired yet? How many men are you going to go through before you realize that *none* of them can meet your deepest needs? I am the only one who can do that!"

The truth is simply this—no human relationship (parent, friend, boyfriend) will ever meet Joy's deepest needs. Every human relationship will fall short and disappoint her! What she needs is JESUS! Keep offering her the love of Christ, pray for her and hopefully she will find real faith and a relationship with Christ before her heart is broken!

Comment On This · Love This · Share with Friends

📝 **Note: Our Hearts.** "God enables us to love. He gives us the greatest treasure in all creation: a heart. For He intends that we should be His intimate allies, to share in the great Romance. Just as we have lost our wonder at the world around us, we have forgotten what a treasure the human heart is. All of the happiness we have ever known and all of the happiness we hope to find is unreachable without a heart. You could not live or love or laugh or cry had God not given you a heart.

And with this heart comes something that staggers me.

God gives us the freedom to reject Him.

He gives to each of us a will of our own.

Good grief, *why*? He knows what free-willed creatures can do. He has already suffered one massive betrayal in the rebellion of the angels. He knows how we will use our freedom, what misery and suffering, what hell will be unleashed on earth because of our choices. *Why?* Is He out of His mind?

The answer is as simple and staggering as this: If you want a world where love is real, you must allow each person the freedom to choose."[4]

 Lynn: I am miserable. My church taught me right from wrong in my early teens, and I vowed not to have sex until I was married. I knew that God loved me, and I knew He wanted me to have a good life. When I started high school, I wanted a boyfriend. This older guy showed interest in me, and I was drawn to him like a magnet. Sadly, I started paying more attention to him than to God. After a couple of months, I had sex with him. Then he graduated and started a job that was apparently more interesting than me, and he broke up with me. I was deceived. I wish I had never gotten so excited about a boyfriend, because this "love" was fake. Only God's love was real, and I'd completely ignored Him. I feel so low and I regret it so much.

Comment On This · Love This · Shares with Friends

 Pam: I'm so sorry for your tremendous pain. You are experiencing a heartache known by many. Dating relationships are in your face. You can see the person and you can hear their words. The hearing and seeing of that relationship is far different than a person's relationship with Christ that is less visual and more experiential. You have to experience who He is and how He loves you through His written Word and moving prayer. And unless you trust in His Word and constantly listen for His voice the voices of the world will drown Him out.

My hope for you today would be that you would trust God with your broken heart. An amazing attribute of God is that He continues to love us no matter how many times we turn our back on Him, thinking that we know what is right or have a better way. This is completely opposite from our human experience where people who feel rejected walk away. Your God has not walked away from you. He hears your cries and longs to bring healing to your soul. Focus on God's love for you. Dig into your Bible. Feel His forgiveness. And remember that it is only when you choose HIM that you will experience a fulfilled life.

Comment On This · Love This · Share with Friends

 Blake: I wish I had heard your message years ago. When I was in high school I was a player. I messed around with girls, thinking that it was no big deal. I was just having "fun." My college roommate invited me to a Christian club event the first week I was on campus. I'd moved a long way from home and was eager to meet some new friends, so I went, even though I'd never been a part of the church. Pam, I was shocked. The room was filled with people my age who thought it was "fun" to worship. It wasn't like anything I'd ever experienced before, so I kept going back. In time I learned about Jesus dying on the cross. He suffered unimaginable pain because He loved ME. I am now a believer and it has changed my life. Because of Him, I want to respect girls and love them right, because someday I want to be married . . . and husbands are to love their wives as Christ loved the church (see Ephesians 5:25).

Comment On This · Love This · Share with Friends

 Pam: I am so encouraged that you have shed our culture's shallow image of cool, to be a cool young man representing Christ. When you experience sex as He designed . . . the "real deal" with your wife . . . it will be far better than you can imagine. Continue to STAND STRONG!

Comment On This · Love This · Share with Friends

📝 **Note: The Promise of Marriage.** "A marriage is not a joining of two worlds, but an abandoning of two worlds in order that one new one might be formed. In this sense, the call to be married can be compared to Jesus' advice to the rich young man to sell all his possessions and to follow Him. It is a vocation to total abandonment. For most people, in fact, marriage is the single most wholehearted step they will ever take toward a fulfillment of Jesus' command to love one's neighbor as oneself. For every marriage partner begins as a neighbor who has been left beaten and wounded on the road of love, whom all the rest of the world has in a sense passed by. What a strange impulse it is that moves us to appreciate the tremendous value of this particular person in a way no other stranger ever has, to the point of committing ourselves totally to them in love, even unto death!"[5]

💟 Kyle's Story

Within a half hour of meeting my wife, Abby, I was intrigued. I started asking her questions and found out that our family structures were very similar. I mean, her parents reminded me so much of my own parents that it was almost scary! The whole time I was thinking, *This girl looks like the type of girl I want to marry.*

I accumulated a bunch of stuff, so I started putting it into a creative memories book. So, we're flipping through the book until she gets to the last page, which has the proposal, and as she's doing that I'm getting down on my knee. She said, "What?" and I flipped open the ring box.

One of the things my sister had told me about when I propose was to make sure that I set it up on a day when we would see a lot of people, because the only thing she'll want to do is show the ring and tell the story. So we're showing the ring and flipping through the book, and the girls are loving the book, and we're calling all around the country to all the different people that we know, and getting pictures. We dated and got engaged all in two-and-a-half months. But when you know, you know.

There are two major things that held me from sexual intercourse until I was 28. I was terrified of getting a girl pregnant. And I was terrified of going home and telling my parents that I had got a girl pregnant.

We both made it all the way until marriage without having sexual intercourse. I made some mistakes in my dating relationships, no doubt. You're wrestling between *just because I love her parts, do I really love her?* And *is this an expression out of love or is it more out of personal desire?* Even after I put on a purity ring and was abstinent until marriage, I made mistakes. Let's be honest. It's a difficult road to walk. Especially with all the things around us that say it's go time. We often aren't really sure if we can stop that freight train once it's in motion. I tried to stay completely away from even going up a girl's shirt because I could not stop that train. I knew that I could not control it, so I needed to set the bar high.

If you make the decision to be abstinent until marriage, and you want to draw that line, you have to draw that line at a place that is really difficult. So, you technically should not want to be physical, because when can you stop that train? You may also find yourself in situations that you probably should not be in, like watching a movie late at night, and it goes into 1 o'clock in the morning and your brain just starts going crazy and you start thinking more with other parts of your anatomy. That becomes a struggle.

We found that a lot of those times when we did slip up it was after midnight or one o'clock in the morning. We should have just gone home. The cool thing about that part of our relationship, where it got really super intense, was when we started to talk about it a lot. Like, "We've got to help each other out because we're struggling physically at the same time, so we've got to hold each other accountable and say we should not go past this line."

The cool thing is that we haven't experienced anything other than each other, and there is peace in that.

Carly: I was flipping through the channels tonight and a tape of your program was on, and it took me back to high school. I don't know if you hear from your success stories, so I wanted to let you know that I followed your advice. My husband and I waited until marriage to have sex, and we have been happily married for five years. We had a lot of support (youth leaders mostly), but hearing your presentation was important to me, because it laid out all of the components on the table and gave me so many reasons to wait. My husband and I are stronger as people and as a couple because we waited and came to know each other so well in that process.

Comment On This · Love This · Shares with Friends

Pam: This made my day! Thank you for the encouragement. I wish you many blessings in your married life.

Comment On This · Love This · Share with Friends

Pam: If you have sex outside of marriage, you will pay. It doesn't matter how old you are. Sex is reserved for one permanent relationship . . . (monogamy does not mean one person at a time). No one has ever had more than one partner and not paid a price.

Comment On This · Love This · Shares with Friends

Chapter 2

Unmasking the Lie:
MGM, MTV and Microsoft—
Who Has Your Attention?

Pam: Whatever has your attention will influence you.

Comment On This · Love This · Shares with Friends

Jill: Pam, I think people overestimate the influence that things we like have on us. For example, I'm drawn into the beat of music, so if it's a good song, I enjoy listening to it and I don't pay much attention to the lyrics. I don't think there is anything wrong with that.

Comment On This · Love This · Share with Friends

Ben: I agree. If I really like a movie, I can tune out the profanity and violence.

Comment On This · Love This · Share with Friends

Pam: I hear this all the time. I also hear, "I am not influenced by the random hookups on *The Real World*. I just like the drama." And, "It doesn't matter that I'm being sexual on IM (instant messaging) and in the chat rooms. I'm not really doing it, so it must be safe." Others confidently claim, "I only look at pornography once in a while. It's not like I'm addicted. Besides, EVERYBODY DOES IT." Sound familiar? Too many of us actually believe that we can spend countless hours with our TVs, on the Internet, watching movies and listening to our iPods and *never be affected*. Not possible.

The battle for our mind is raging all around us, all the time. Are we going to fight this battle or just give in and let the enemy win? This is a call to arms. A call to step up to the plate—to actually do something and not just sit there and let the "culture" influence our thoughts, attitudes, values and behavior. Make no mistake. What goes "in" *will always* find its way "out." We must take a long, honest look at what we are putting into our minds and hearts. How much time are we spending with the media, and how is it shaping our values? The battle cannot be won if we do not first acknowledge it needs to be fought, then understand the enemy's tactics and, finally, arm ourselves for the fight.

Comment On This · Love This · Share with Friends

📌 **Note: The Battle Is On.** Satan wants your soul, but to get it he must first have your mind. Since the beginning of time, Satan has been the great deceiver. And, amazingly, with very little change to his basic tactics, he continues to succeed on a regular basis. Are we really that stupid?

In Genesis 3, we see Satan, the serpent, approach Eve and ask her the same question he has been asking every soul since that day. "Did God really say, 'You must not eat from any tree in the garden'?" (v. 1) Through that question, he asked Eve to second-guess God's commands, His plan and His design.

We continue to see this struggle in our everyday world. In today's society, questioning authority, boundaries and the purpose of the "rules" is a constant theme of music and pop culture. The "It's my life . . . it's my body . . . it's my choice" mantra is repeated over and over. Sadly, we've gotten to a place where many people think, *Who does God think He is to tell me how to live my life?*

For those who are smart enough to recognize the goodness of God's design and the boundaries He has set, Satan will move on to tactic number two. This one almost always works if the first ploy fails. When Eve replied to the serpent, "God did say, 'You must not eat fruit [not "any"—Satan likes to exaggerate the rule] from the tree that is in the middle of the garden . . . or you will die'" (v. 3). Satan laughed, making her feel naive and completely gullible. Then he said, "You will surely not die . . . For God knows that if you eat of that tree, you will be as wise as He is—and He certainly doesn't want that!" (vv. 4-5, author's paraphrase).

Basically, Satan uses the "God's holding out on you" tactic. He tries to get you to believe that God doesn't really care about your best interests; he twists God's goodness into ruining your fun. Eve fell for this lie. Distrusting God's love for her, she ate the apple, and you know the rest of the story. The result was lifelong pain. We *must* recognize the battle and be on guard!

Jade: I'm a virgin, but I want to have sex really badly. What should I do?

Comment On This · Love This · Shares with Friends

Pam: Typically, when we are struggling with sexual feelings and temptation, it is because of what we are putting into our MIND. Your most important sex organ is *not* covered by your swimsuit. *It is your mind.* Please pay close attention to what you are listening to, reading, looking at and watching on TV and in the movies. Sexual arousal does not come from a vapor. It is triggered by what we hear and what we see! I would advise cutting out *everything* in your life that is causing you to want to make bad choices! This will help you avoid temptation.

Comment On This · Love This · Share with Friends

Brynn: I've been with my boyfriend for a few years. We haven't had actual sex, but sometimes we have phone sex, and I text him naked pictures. Sometimes I'm not really in the mood, but he kind of pressures me. After reading your post I'm feeling like I'm wrong for sexting, even though it's not the "real thing."

Comment On This · Love This · Shares with Friends

Pam: "Phone sex" is very serious. I know that sometimes it is easy to justify participating in sexual talk on the phone or on the Internet because you aren't actually "doing it," and that seems to make it safe (you certainly wouldn't get a disease or get pregnant). But, there is no question that participating in this behavior causes sexual arousal, and eventually it is followed by actual sex. It is usually just a matter of time.

The pictures only fuel the fire in the temptation to have sex. You are *showing him* what is intended to be kept secret, and there is a reason for that—God knew that exposing our bodies *increases* the desire for touch and intimacy. So, you are showing him your body from a distance and inducing this effect from afar, and yet you expect him to respect a safe boundary when he is around you?! That makes no sense. Of course he is going to want to act on what you have shown and "given" to him already. If you want to be respected, you will have to protect the purity of his mind, *not fill it with your sexual imagery*. Furthermore, teens across the country are getting in trouble with the law, as in facing criminal charges, for taking, sending and looking at these pictures.[1] It is child pornography!

The fact that your conscience is telling you this isn't good seems to be a *giant red flag*. Now you have a choice. You can listen to your conscience and stop the behavior to find out what this relationship is really about (if he breaks up because you won't do this anymore you'll know he doesn't care about you, just what he can get *from* you). Or, you can continue to ignore your conscience and risk moving closer and closer to doing more things that you will most certainly regret. I hope you will listen to the voice telling you to stop sexting and regain your purity.

Comment On This · Love This · Share with Friends

Newsflash: Sexting—20 percent of teens have sent or posted nude/semi-nude pictures or videos of themselves.[2]

Pam: Sometimes we think that our sins committed in secret won't matter. But, if we don't take care of them, it will destroy our lives.

Comment On This · Love This · Shares with Friends

Max: I'm struggling with pornography. I want to get away from it because I'm realizing how it is already affecting me. There is this girl that I've started dating, and she wants to have sex. Now I'm really trying to get away from the relationship. The images have made me so curious and excited that when she is saying, "I feel ready to have sex," I want to do it. But I've grown up believing that sex belongs in marriage. This is so hard.

Comment On This · Love This · Share with Friends

Pam: A big part of the battle is *recognizing* that you are weak and need help! Sometimes when we think we are strong enough we don't take the necessary steps to protect ourselves from falling into temptation.

First things first: Until you get this pornography problem under control, you are definitely not ready for a dating relationship with ANY girl! Whether you like it or not, the reality is that you *attract* what you *are*. So, if your personal life is not in order (no matter how private you might think it is), you are certainly going to attract the *wrong* girl. Knowing that, I would encourage you to take time to work on *you*! One huge practical suggestion is to figure out *when* and *where* you are struggling with the most temptation and *avoid* these situations—movies, books, the Internet or whatever it is that is causing you to fall. Then, fill that "free time" with more *positive* activities and relationships! Keep yourself *busy* doing *good things*!

Comment On This · Love This · Share with Friends

📰 **Newsflash:** The average teen spends 1 hour and 40 minutes per week browsing for pornography.[3]

📝 **Note: No One Is Immune.** Check out this amazing testimony from popular Christian singer Clay Crosse about the impact pornography had on him from his childhood years all the way into his marriage. His story is a powerful reminder that no one is immune. We must keep our eyes and ears away from anything that doesn't honor God!

He saw [pornographic images] for the first time when he was in the fourth grade, and couldn't believe his eyes. Years later, he saw them again, and by the time he was in high school, he had a few tucked away in his bedroom.

"No one ever told me those images would burn themselves into my mind and come back to haunt me," wrote Christian music artist Clay Crosse in *I Surrender All: Rebuilding a Marriage Broken by Pornography*. Clay coauthored the book with his wife Renee and author Mark Tabb.

Little did he know that his boyhood fascination with pictures of naked women would resurface in his dating life and later in his marriage when he was at the pinnacle of his Christian music career. . . .

Clay and Renee began dating at a young age and knew early on that they were meant to be together. They both grew up in Christian homes and made public commitments to sexual purity, although Clay admits that Renee's commitment was much stronger than his. Growing impatient, Clay began viewing pornography as a "safe" release for his lust.

"I always equated purity with not having sex, and since I'd not had sex, I thought I was doing okay," Clay wrote. "I liked the feeling lust built up inside me, and I could get it quickly with porn. All the while I told myself, *Well, at least Renee and I aren't sleeping together.*"

Clay and Renee made it to their wedding day without having sex. Clay saw this day as a fresh start and assumed his struggle with lust and pornography was over since he no longer "needed" pornographic images for sexual release.

"I threw out any traces of pornography and vowed to walk away from it, never to return," Clay wrote. "But the damage of pornography doesn't end when the video stops or the magazine is thrown away."

The couple learned this the hard way.[4]

Erin: This story brought tears to my eyes. I had no idea that Clay Crosse struggled with this evil . . . and I was shocked! I've always liked his music. What a powerful testimony. I'm thankful that through his story he can articulate how the influence of a simple childhood glance can grow into something that damages sweethearts that were trying to honor God. Wow.

Comment On This · Love This · Share with Friends

James: I had no idea that pornography could do this. I've never heard it explained this way.

Comment On This · Love This · Share with Friends

Chelsea: It is great that he acknowledged the truth and supported his wife. I'm kind of surprised she stayed. It must have been hard to hear that. After reading this, I really hope—in a new way—that my future spouse is protecting his eyes!

Comment On This · Love This · Share with Friends

Pam: It is a powerful story! Chelsea, Clay's wife, Renee, was obviously devastated. Her response is one that shows true dependence on God. She was understandably hurt and yet she didn't harden her heart and walk away. She prayed over her husband and together they have written a book sharing their story in hopes of helping others. They also have a ministry called Holy Homes that encourages and strengthens Christ-based marriages and families. I pray that through this platform many will be touched and recognize the incredibly destructive power of sexual imagery.
Comment On This · Love This · Share with Friends

 Pam: Who has your attention today—God or the lie?
Comment On This · Love This · Shares with Friends

📝 Note: Know the Real Deal

I was once told that FBI agents who are trained to detect counterfeit money spend most of their training time studying the real thing. Considering it wasted energy to study every possible way that money could be counterfeited, the primary purpose of their training is to teach them so incredibly well what real money looks like that the minute something counterfeit is put in front of them they will immediately recognize it.

This principle holds true to God's truth versus Satan's lies. We don't need to spend hours and hours studying every way the enemy brings lies into our lives. Rather, we need to spend hours and hours studying the *truth* so that the minute we see or hear something contrary to truth, we immediately recognize it as a lie.

Here's the problem. The average student is spending upward of 20 hours a week with the *lie* and, dare I suggest, *far less* with the *truth!* [5] Even if you count Sunday morning church services and a weekly youth group meeting, you are looking at less than one-tenth of the time you spend with media. And that is assuming you actually pay attention during those times.

My godly grandfather, who is now with Jesus, taught me a poem when I was a little girl. I never understood the poem until I was much older; now its message seems so clear!

> Vice is a monster of so fearful a mien;
> As to be hated, upon merely being seen.
> But seen too oft, familiar with its faces;
> One first endures, then fondles, then embraces.
> (Author unknown)

How has the time you've spent with "monster" vice dulled your conscience? Be honest. Have you felt that tug at your conscience recently? Or have you ignored it so long and gotten so used to seeing the monster that he doesn't seem so ugly? Have you actually gotten so far down the path that you now have this monster as your pet?

Carl: Your latest posts and status update have me thinking. I met this girl online. My friend told me about this chat room that he stumbled upon and "met" some cool people. I decided to check it out and starting chatting with this girl. She seemed cool. We both like soccer and can't wait to be done with high school. It felt like we connected, and we started making plans to be on the computer at the same time to instant message. At first everything was innocent. But she doesn't live here. I've never seen her. In some ways she doesn't seem real. Neither one of us was dating, but we both wanted to be and we started cyber-flirting. Our words were sexually suggestive and we mentally acted like we were doing things. Cyber sex, I guess you could call it. Is that real sex? Would you call it "dangerous"? We kind of want to meet.

Comment On This · Love This · Shares with Friends

Pam: Your questions are good ones. You have fallen into a trap that has hurt many people. Since you are conversing through a computer . . . basically a box . . . you think you can do or say anything. But even if she doesn't seem real, she is real. And because you two have allowed yourself to walk down a dangerous mental road, your conscience—your ability to determine right from wrong—is clouded. Satan has you right where he wants you.

Because the word "cybersex" ends in "sex," it is obvious that it is a form of sex, although it is different from physical sex. Obviously there is no genital contact to run the risk of pregnancy or an STD. But in a very real and powerful way it *is* spiritual and emotional sex. It draws two people together through explicit sexual language and bodily response. This is not healthy. Not only does it take the focus off of purity and God's design for sex, but it also demeans the beauty and gift of the body through sexual bonding. Carrying over into "real" relationships, this lack of respect for someone on the computer will likely result in a lack of patience for sex with a girlfriend.

Do not go visit this girl. Through your words and mental imagery you have unlocked a powerful drive that will be *very real* if you see each other face to face. Rather, you need to open your Bible. Today you have a choice. You can continue on this dangerous path or you can refocus on Christ. *Look* at what He has to say about the holiness of the body. Look at what He has to say about temptation. Look at what He says to you about love. If you do not take the time to do this, Carl, your relationships are only going to invite pain.

Remember the words of Ephesians 6:10-11: "Finally, be strong in the Lord and in his mighty power. Put on the full armor of God so that you can take your stand against the devil's schemes."

Comment On This · Love This · Share with Friends

💜 Katherine's Story

My father was one of my best friends. When he died five years ago, I felt lonely and empty. To fill the emptiness, I sought "love." I went online and interacted with this boy that I thought was 17, for around 20 minutes. Then I gave him my phone number and he gave me his. We started talking on the phone a few hours later and he said I sounded interesting. A few days later he said that he liked me. I was 14 years old at the time.

I invited him over, knowing it wasn't a good idea but still did it anyway. We were speaking for two weeks or so, talking for almost an hour or two every night/day. One night he came over. He said I was adorable and cute. He started touching me and holding me, which I really liked. I liked the attention. Then he took me into my garage and had sex with me.

He abused me during sex. He pushed me down to the floor, shook me and said, "Why? Why can't we just have sex? You invited me over." The reason I invited him over is because I liked the attention he gave me. He kissed me, held me close, looked in my eyes and said how beautiful I was.

After six months of knowing him, he confronted me, saying he was 30. I freaked. I had fallen for him, I thought, like teenage love. Even after I found out that he was 30, he still picked me up from school and took me to his condo. I learned that you can't always trust people by the way they act or show themselves.

I am now 16 years old. It's been a year since everything went down with the guy who abused me. It took months to realize that I was accountable for half of what happened. I understand I am not a victim, but at the same time I had to realize it was not my fault that I was being manipulated and physically hurt. This guy picked on the easiest target, which then was me—a weak young teen. He is now in jail.

What I got was not love or positive attention. I was slowly getting eaten up inside. I was crumbling, not noticing that anything huge was going on. The thing that has hurt me the most is that I lost my virginity to a sex offender, someone I easily trusted a year ago because I so badly was grasping the attention I wanted. That is all I cared about then.

I hope many teens realize that your virginity is one of the most important things. It's a gift to give your partner to show your love. I wear a ring around my ring finger stating that I am waiting until I KNOW that person is the one. The feeling of love will be amazing.

I know my life won't be a fairytale. But I want the happy ending that many people do. I realize that God has given me a second chance to life. I do not, at this point, have any STDs. I am grateful. I took the wrong path but He gave me choices, and with the support of my family and friends I got the help I needed.

After spending months at an intense residential treatment center, I am back home where I am starting out new and fresh at a new school with new relationships. I hope people realize that even through the worst times in life they can pull themselves up— they can get the help they need, and nothing will stop them. I want people to know to never give up. Life only gives you one chance—a chance to fulfill your dreams and make a difference—don't ruin it over peer pressure or insecurities! I wake up every morning with a smile on my face and thank God for waking me up and giving me a chance to live again.

Pam: "The devil plants a seed in our mind, but we water it, fertilize it, prune it and help it to grow" (author unknown).

Comment On This · Love This · Shares with Friends

Elana: What a cool quote. The world is just so full of pressures, and it can be difficult to know what is right. Are there some Scriptures that you could point me to for direction?

Comment On This · Love This · Share with Friends

Pam: Good question. You need to arm yourself for the battle. This is not going to be easy, but it might be the most important battle you fight. If you win on the battlefield of your *mind*, purity in your actions will be much easier. Here are some Scriptures you can put in your mind's memory bank that will help you!

> I will refuse to look at anything vile and vulgar. I hate all who deal crookedly; I will have nothing to do with them (Psalm 101:3, *NLT*).

> Finally, brothers, whatever is true, whatever is noble, whatever is right, whatever is pure, whatever is lovely, whatever is admirable—if anything is excellent or praiseworthy—think about such things (Philippians 4:8).

Comment On This · Love This · Share with Friends

Amy: My biggest struggle with Satan and the media today is not a temptation to devalue others, but that it has fed a chronic dissatisfaction and undervaluing of my own body. It makes women feel like they cannot measure up. Body image is crummy unless you are a size two or four. How many fit that image?! This leads to thoughts of inadequacy and questions of worth. Praise the Lord that He looks way beyond the label on my jeans and the size of my hips.

Comment On This · Love This · Share with Friends

Pam: Amen to that! I find it interesting that as women we are constantly measuring ourselves against an unhealthy ideal. Hollywood stars and models are deemed "perfect" in our mind, but did you know that the average runway model has a body mass index (BMI) of only 16?[6] A BMI of 16! Yet, the CDC says a healthy BMI is 18.5 to 24.9.[7] We need to let the image go!

Beyond the scale, we need to remember that God calls our bodies a *temple*. While Satan wants us to believe that we will have a "better" life if we weigh less, this isn't about numbers. Our value cannot be found in the bathroom scale's results, and our happiness will never be attained through outward appearance. It will never be "enough," because we live in a society with a constantly changing perspective on beauty and fulfillment.

God does not change. And He says, "Do you not know that your body is a temple of the Holy Spirit, who is in you, whom you have received from God? You are not your own" (1 Corinthians 6:19). This means that when God fashioned the world, He fashioned you, and He took great care in your creation and called your body "holy." The point, then, is not to "measure up" to some limitless ideal but to remember whose you are and honor God by being healthy. Fulfillment in both your body and life circumstances will come if you trust in His love. Release yourself from Satan's lie and take a look in the mirror to see the beauty that He created and loves.

Comment On This · Love This · Share with Friends

👣 Sara's Story

It was the beginning of my freshman year of high school. And with a somewhat new crowd of people, I felt insecure in myself. What activities do I get involved in to use my God-given gifts for His glory? Who are my true friends? How come some girls can just be friends with guys, but I can't? And am I good enough to have a boyfriend, because I haven't in the past?

It seemed obvious for me at the time to start with the outward appearance! That's what gives people their first impression, right? And the lies started there. Through my eyes, the skinny, pretty girls were the ones in the limelight on the drama team, getting solos in the choir, starring on the volleyball or basketball court and hanging out with their boyfriends in the hallway between classes and after school. In other words, the girls that looked like all the starring roles in all the movies seemed to have all the fun, get all the attention, and I didn't look like them!

I knew I didn't meet up to the "ideal" figure in society, Hollywood or even my own small town for that matter. So, I figured I'd better lose a couple pounds. I wasn't fat, but I surely wasn't skinny either. The weight started coming off and people starting noticing. In the meantime, other things happened in my life that were out of my control. Adding these factors together made for a budding eating disorder called anorexia to give me some control in my life.

If only it was as simple as that to uncover in the beginning. If only my eyes had been open to the warnings and insights God was trying to teach me. But no, I fed into the lies of society from Satan rather than rely on God's truths from the Bible. My struggle was long and hard and affected many people around me for years to come. It took many hours of prayer, counseling sessions, trips to the doctor's and dietician's office, an extended hospital stay four hours from home at one point and the devotion and support of an amazing family, friends and church family.

With society focusing strictly on the weight issue, it made the process drag out, and it was more difficult to address the core issues because it appeared that all I had to do was eat and everything would be better. After a five-year journey focused on weight and control, I experienced God's gift of grace, healing mercies and forgiveness like I never had before. This whole process and self-focused addiction of food and exercise was because of distrust in a sovereign Father God. I failed to remember that He desired a personal relationship with me no matter how imperfect I was, and that the Creator of the Universe is and always will be in control, no matter what the situation.

I had only seen myself as someone who couldn't achieve perfection; but as God's child, He loves me just as I am! I needed to take time to hear that my body was not my own, but a temple of the living God, created to honor Him in every way (see 1 Corinthians 6:19-20). And with my eating disorder, I could not serve two masters—I could not serve both God and food. In order to be fully used for His purpose and revel in my Savior's immense love for me, I had to give up the fight and allow God to take over, because "[He] is able to do immeasurably more than all we ask or imagine, according to his power that is at work within us, to him be the glory in the church and in Christ Jesus throughout all generations, for ever and ever! Amen" (Ephesians 3:20-21).

@ **Link:** Hey, girls! A girlfriend posted a link to "More Beautiful You" by Jonny Diaz on her page, and I wanted to encourage you to look it up. (You can also find the link on the *Nobody Told Me* Facebook fan page.) Remember, you can never find value or assess beauty through the eyes of the world. God made you with a purpose, and because He handcrafted you, you are beautiful!

Kendra: Cool! I love it!
Comment On This · Love This · Share with Friends

Pam: Jonny actually wrote this song because of the lie that culture drives, defining beauty and image that opposes God's Word. It is really great for both genders because the media influences the self-worth and action of boys and girls. IGNORE Satan! "There could never be a more beautiful you."
Comment On This · Love This · Share with Friends

 Jacqueline: The devil is a filthy liar.
Comment On This · Love This · Share with Friends

 Pam: You got that right. And he's a powerful one. No one said holiness was easy. Nothing worth having comes without a price. We all want to "win the gold" but no one wants the hours of sacrifice and training it takes to be the best! Make no mistake, this is hardcore training. We are conditioning the muscles of our character. I think we have all believed that if we were faced with the fiery furnace, as Shadrach, Meshach and Abednego were (read about it in Daniel 3), we would stand up to King Nebuchadnezzar and tell him to take his silly law and shove it, even if it meant we would be burned to a crisp! The problem is, we think we will stand when the "big test" comes, but we fail to stand in the everyday simple tests. What makes you think you can bench press 150 lbs. if you have never lifted a 5 lb. dumbbell? Knowing that the devil's lies are powerful demands knowing truth so that we don't make choices we regret.
Comment On This · Love This · Share with Friends

📝 **Note: Toe Fungus.** Whenever I want to more clearly envision the "monster" of impure thoughts and remind myself of the battle I have to fight daily, I think of that commercial on TV that never ceases to gross me out. The one with the gross toe fungal yellow monsters they say live under my toenails . . . ughhhh! I want them *out*. Whatever the cost! And I know it's hard. You may be wounded in the process, but pick yourself up, confess your failure, pray for strength and battle on! The *prize* is worth it!

 Layton: That commercial is disgusting! I've never thought of it in relationship to my faith life or purity of mind, but it makes sense!
Comment On This · Love This · Share with Friends

 Teegan: Thanks for the personal reminder at the end. I so want to please my heavenly Father; and because I do, I need to be carefully thinking through every message I'm putting into my brain.
Comment On This · Love This · Share with Friends

Pam: Your heavenly Father loves you, and He will always be better than the "stuff" of the world to prove to yourself that you're attractive. And since, for young ladies, attractiveness and self-esteem are linked so strongly, it's like we try to validate our entire self-worth in that way, by doing something that degrades it. The devil is such a filthy liar, eh?

Comment On This · Love This · Share with Friends

 Janessa: Thank you for challenging us to let go of sin and refocus on Christ. I've made some bad choices. I know it. But you have reminded me that I don't have to let sin and filth live there forever. I can confess it and then choose to make sure that everything I intentionally put in my mind is of God so that all that flows out of me from now on honors Him. I don't want a damaged future. I don't want to buy the lie. I want honest joy and holiness.

Comment On This · Love This · Shares with Friends

 Pam: GOOD FOR YOU! When temptation strikes, *never forget this feeling*!

Comment On This · Love This · Share with Friends

 Pam: Temptation will come, and come often. The difference is how you deal with temptation. Are you fighting it, battling for purity of mind? Or have you thrown up your hands in despair and allowed the monster to make its home permanently in your mind and soul?

Comment On This · Love This · Shares with Friends

Chapter 3

The Lies Get Personal: Peers and Partners

 Pam: "Show me your friends and I'll show you your future" (author unknown).
Comment On This · Love This · Shares with Friends

 Jake: What do you mean?
Comment On This · Love This · Share with Friends

 Brittany: I'm a virgin, and I am dating a guy that isn't. Before we started dating he had several partners. I've always been one that easily said no to sex, but recently my two best friends lost their virginity. Now I feel like I have no one to talk to. I listen to them talk and they have no idea what it's like to be the only one that is a virgin. I know my boyfriend would do it, and I don't know how much longer I can take this. I totally get this.
Comment On This · Love This · Share with Friends

 Lee: Some people might cave into their friends' habits, but my parents always taught me to be a leader and not a follower. If I know what I believe and follow through with that, it won't matter who I hang out with. I can be my own person!
Comment On This · Love This · Share with Friends

 Pam: Lee, you definitely need to think more about this. The influence of the people we spend the most time with, the people we share our hearts with, the people we consider our closest friends, cannot be underestimated. It is so important that we *choose* our friends, not just let them "choose" us. This implies that we are being *deliberate* about who we spend time with.

Brittany, you are not alone. We ALL have a need to belong. Let's be honest here! Nobody wants to be the outcast! We long to feel accepted and worthy. And sometimes, because of this need, we begin to abandon our own personal values and identity. Through a little compromise here and a big sacrifice there, our true self is abandoned. If this goes on for too long, we wake up one day and stand before the mirror completely unable to recognize the person reflected back. We have "lost" ourselves to fit the mold of those around us. Once believing that we were "strong enough" to be different than our friends or that we would be the person to "change them," we ultimately find ourselves the one who wound up changed.

Comment On This · Love This · Share with Friends

 Lisa: I saw your video and was instantly inspired to save sex for marriage. Like you, I think that serious relationships in high school are crazy. But the truth is that I can't think of one of my friends who hasn't at least had oral sex. They aren't even in serious relationships. It's just something "fun" to do. They say things to me like, "You'll understand when you get a boyfriend. Right now you are too inexperienced." I always feel weird and left out. Do you think that teens should date someone that they could see themselves marrying or, at this point in my life, should I just be dating for experience? Should I get a new group of friends? Please help me. I know I should feel okay about it because I have respect for myself, but the truth is that I feel horrible.

Comment On This · Love This · Shares with Friends

 Pam: I'm so glad that you wrote me. First, let me say that oral sex is serious. Your friends might think these random hookups are "fun," but this type of "fun" can lead to the spread of STDs; and last time I checked no one thought having a sexually transmitted disease was "fun." In fact, most infected people that I've talked to use words like "horrifying," "embarrassing" and "depressing."

Setting your standards high is the *right* way to date. You don't just want to date for "experience," because that would mean that you are dating anyone that asks and participating in behaviors that you know aren't safe or healthy. You are better than that.

I find the whole "experience" thing comical. How exactly do your friends think this experience is going to help them? What do they think their future husband will say to this: "Honey, guess what? I built up my marriage résumé through sexual relations with other people! I got HPV, and you'll get it too, but at least I'll know what I'm doing"? Do you think that future mate will say, "Good . . . I'm so excited! I know that sex is really complicated, so it's a good thing you've taken time to practice and share yourself with others so that I can share our marriage bed with them too . . . THANK YOU"? I highly doubt it! This "experience" is only going to bring pain. Guaranteed.

Lisa, on *any day* you could choose to be like your friends, but *never again* can they be like you. You have something special.

If your friends are harassing you, they aren't acting like good friends. Pray about this.

It's challenging enough to spend time with people who don't share our likes and morals, let alone be close friends with them. You will certainly feel more at peace if you are spending time with people who like to do the same things you do and share your value system, because you won't have to "work" to fit in. The reality is this: If *all* of your friends are having sex, it will be extremely difficult to keep your commitment to purity, because you will always feel like the odd one out.

Comment On This · Love This · Share with Friends

💕 Kala's Story

Recently, I attended one of your high school assemblies. You saved my life that day.

All of my friends are having sex. They brag about it and discuss their sex lives right in front of me all the time, even though they know I've never had sex. Naturally, it makes me feel completely left out.

I decided that I was going to do something about that. I would just get it over with. Then I would have my own story to share, and I could giggle and gossip right along with them.

I wasn't dating anyone at the time, so I asked a friend if he'd be willing to have sex. I assured him that there would be no strings attached and that I wouldn't expect any kind of continued relationship with him. He agreed, and we set up an "appointment" for Friday after school.

You were at my school on a Wednesday, and you saved me from making the worst decision of my life. If you had come the next week, I might have compromised everything just to fit in—myself, my health, my education, my future marriage and my ability to have children. I might have reduced the gift and beauty of sex to a simple appointment in my date book. I get teary just thinking about it.

I cancelled my plans and decided that if my friends kept pressuring me I would find new ones.

 Asher: I am an 18-year-old boy who is a virgin, but I feel very stressed about what to do. My friends have all had sex and, while they are great guys most of the time, it is really hard when they start talking about these relationships. They think that what they are doing is "normal." Is it? I'm headed off to college and I really want to stay a virgin until I'm married, but the world is full of people who want it for the wrong meaning, and I'm afraid of the temptation. I would love some advice.

Comment On This · Love This · Shares with Friends

Pam: First of all let me say GOOD FOR YOU! You are making the right choice and you should be proud of yourself. You are building *strong character!* When you choose sexual purity you are not at risk for the physical, emotional or spiritual consequences that face those who choose to have sex before marriage. The *best* and most *meaningful* sex is shared between two individuals who have saved themselves for each other.

Your friends are not making a "normal" choice. I've met thousands of students across this country and worldwide who have chosen abstinence. What appears to be "popular" does not make it *right!*

I want to encourage you with some Scripture. God's Word is always true!

Let those who love the Lord hate evil, for he guards the lives of his faithful ones and delivers them from the hand of the wicked (Psalm 97:10).

Do not let your heart envy sinners, but always be zealous for the fear of the Lord (Proverbs 23:17).

In fact, everyone who wants to live a godly life in Christ Jesus will be persecuted (2 Timothy 3:12).

No temptation has seized you except what is common to man. And God is faithful; he will not let you be tempted beyond what you can bear. But when you are tempted, he will also provide a way out so that you can stand up under it (1 Corinthians 10:13).

Keep standing strong, Asher!

Comment On This · Love This · Share with Friends

 Pam: "Peer pressure": n. Pressure from one's peers to behave in a manner similar or acceptable to them.[1] Are you standing strong, or will you cave in?

Comment On This · Love This · Shares with Friends

 Logan: Reading your status update has me stressed. I have the most wonderful girlfriend in the world and I love her more than anything. And I would do anything to keep us together; but lately she has been talking about how she thinks she is ready for us to have sex. I'm not sure what to do because we are only 15, but I really just want to be with her forever. Maybe I should just offer to sleep in the same place, and only sleep. Do you think that would be a bad plan?

Comment On This · Love This · Share with Friends

 Pam: YES! Two points to remember about sleeping in the same place: (1) You would be putting yourself (and her) in a place of temptation *way* beyond what you can control. Can you get into the fireplace, start the fire and not get burned? (2) If you are asking a *moral* question, Ephesians 5:3 says, "But among you there must not be even a hint of sexual immorality, or of any kind of impurity, or of greed, because these are improper for God's holy people." I take this to mean, "It's better to not even *look* like that's what you're doing!" Your reputation *matters*!

I know that you really care about this girl and you think you would like to be with her forever, but it sure seems like the two of you do *not* hold the same values. She might just be *using* you to meet her own selfish desires. You deserve better than that. Take some time away from the relationship to focus on other friendships and your *own* character for a while, and really think through the inner qualities that you want in your spouse so that you can be *selective* about the people you date in the future.

Make sure you take time to evaluate your own values and boundaries. Do you know what they are? Have you talked them over with a parent or an adult mentor? Can you clearly communicate your values to someone else? If any of your answers are *no,* you need to back up and get this right! Every single time I have heard people tell me the story of being pressured into having sex, they eventually admit they never really made their boundaries clear.

Comment On This · Love This · Share with Friends

Note: When Are You Ready to Date? As difficult as it might be to fight off pressure from your friends, it is far more difficult to fight off temptation when you are in a relationship. No matter how much you try to keep your head in charge, your heart is prone to taking over. This is why it is so important to know who you are, what you value and what you intend not to do before you get into a dating relationship. This is one reason that I suggest not dating before age 16. Until then you are more susceptible to pressure from peers and specifically from people older or more experienced than you.

This is not just "this old lady's opinion." In most every state, we have "age of consent" laws stating that people under 16 (in some states it is 15) are incapable of giving "consent" to sexual behavior. That sounds very "legal," but the point is that if you are not 16, you do not have the "resources" (maturity) to consent to sex.

I am in no way saying that I believe 16 is a magic age. There are some 16-year-olds who are still unable to understand the consequences of sex and, therefore, are incapable of making good decisions in relationships. That is why it is so important for parents and caring adults to evaluate not just your age but also your maturity and the strength of your conviction. Do you have the ability to say *no*? If not, then you are certainly not ready to date.

Another good rule is to never date anyone who is more than a year older or younger than you. After you reach your twenties, you could change that rule a bit; but prior to your twenties, age gaps indicate huge maturity differences. Most seniors can drive, are registered to vote and are considering where to go to college to study for their career. Freshman and sophomores, on the other hand, are just learning their way around the school hallways and adjusting to high school life. And if they are out of high school they are legally an adult, many of them living on their own and beginning to experience life outside of the watchful eye of a parent. To believe that you could really be "in love" when you are in such completely different phases of life is deception, and you are inviting a lot of pain!

Dori: I always wondered why you say age 16 in your talk. Thanks for the explanation!

Comment On This · Love This · Share with Friends

Marren: I'm 14, and I recently made a mistake. I didn't have sex with my boyfriend, but I allowed him to pressure me into removing my shirt and bra. I'm not sure how I let myself get into the situation, and I regret it so much. I feel dirty even though I told him I'm fine.

Comment On This · Love This · Share with Friends

Pam: Marren's honesty raises another key point to mature dating. Before you get into *any* relationship you need to clearly communicate your personal values and boundaries on the *first date,* as well as know and state what the consequences will be if those boundaries are pressed or broken. You cannot just "go with the flow" to see what happens, nor can you expect them to just "know" where your boundary line is!

Once you have clearly communicated your values and boundaries for any physical relationship, you must *stick to it!* Words mean nothing if they are not followed by actions. Anyone can *say* they have values. You have to *prove* your values by the way you live. Don't *tell* me what you believe; *show me!* Your values will be made clear by your actions. If a date tells you he *values* purity and wants to keep his relationship with you pure, but the first time you are alone he has his hands all over you, there should be a "red flag" that screams "LIAR!" And if you state at the beginning of the relationship where your "line" is, and one month into the relationship you have moved the line, then you are not serious about your values. It is not about what you say. It is about what you DO!

Comment On This · Love This · Share with Friends

Lianne: My boyfriend is three years older than me. Today we talked about sex and I explained that I don't want to have sex before marriage. Then he said that I didn't give him a good enough excuse why we shouldn't do it and hung up on me.

Comment On This · Love This · Shares with Friends

 Pam: KICK HIM TO THE CURB! You should *never* have to justify to a date why you do not want to have sex outside of marriage. You should communicate your standards, but you shouldn't have to "fight" to defend yourself. *Anyone* who pushes you to change your standards clearly doesn't really care about you. He is trying to see what he can "get" from you. (This can be true of a girl as well.) The boundary speaks for itself, and any guy who truly loves you will honor it.

Comment On This · Love This · Share with Friends

💔 Victoria's Story

 I never dated all through high school, and when I got to college, I started hanging out with one guy. Quickly I developed a huge crush on him.

For our first date we went to see the *Exorcist*. This should have been a clue to me that he wasn't the quality that I thought he was. Following the movie we went to eat. It seemed like a pretty good first date, and I was excited for the second.

A week later we went to the river. I wanted to walk next to the river; he wanted to get in the back seat. He talked me into his plans. I didn't see what it could really hurt. I was hoping my first kiss would be from him, and here was my chance. So he kissed me, but he didn't stop. He kept pushing and pushing me to go further. He got further that night than I ever thought I would let a guy go before I got married. I was so confused.

The next week, I made the conscious decision that I would be fine with us spending the night in a hotel. He told me that I would be the same the next day, implying that we wouldn't sleep together. We just wanted to spend some real time together where we could act like a couple and make out. I met him that night. I knew it was wrong, but I didn't care. He made me feel good about myself, and the secretive romance was very appealing. I trusted him.

I went to the hotel with him a week or so later. The morning after, he told me that I needed to take the "morning after pill" to ensure that I didn't get pregnant. I obliged. Those pills not only may have killed a life, but they forever changed my life. Everything in me wanted to die. I saw no sign of hope. I was in such a deep depression.

I knew that sex was wrong, and I knew what kind of consequences there would be, but I thought I was in love. It didn't seem like such a bad idea. But I never knew a heart could truly feel like it was ripped in two.

Pam: Alcohol and "making right choices" *never* mix. Nothing will kill your chances of staying pure faster than drinking!

Comment On This · Love This · Shares with Friends

Cianne: My boyfriend and I made a promise to save our virginity for our wedding night. Well, he got drunk one night and some chick took advantage of him, and they ended up having sex. It tore me up, but I don't blame him.

Comment On This · Love This · Share with Friends

Pam: Back up. What this boy did was *his* decision and *his* responsibility. He *chose* to drink, and everyone knows that drinking impairs judgment. Therefore, he put himself in a dangerous situation. You can't completely blame the girl. That wouldn't fly in a marriage. It doesn't fly now. There will always be girls (someday women) who will "throw" themselves at boys, but this does not justify the sex. He should have *run* in the other direction! And he needs to be tested for STDs. He has put *any* future partner at risk for infection.

I think you need to take a step back from this and all dating relationships until you better understand healthy boundaries for *both* people involved in a relationship. If you settle for "anything goes" now, you will have to be okay with it later too. Is that what you want?

Comment On This · Love This · Share with Friends

Jake: I went to a party with my friends and they were all having sex. I'd had a little to drink and I didn't want to be the odd man out, so I ended up cheating on my girlfriend. I'm afraid to tell her because I'm afraid she'll break up with me. Do I need to?

Comment On This · Love This · Share with Friends

Pam: *Of course* you need to tell her. She deserves to know the truth! Relationships should be built on honesty and respect, and that should be afforded to her just like you would want it for yourself. Will it hurt her? Yes. Will the relationship end? I don't know. But doing the right thing and proving that you value honesty is far more important. Withholding the *truth* about your failure will only prolong the pain. But remember, *trust is earned.* Since you have violated trust, it will likely take a very long time to prove to her that you have changed and can be trusted in the future.

Comment On This · Love This · Share with Friends

@ Link: Are you thinking that you don't want to be the "odd one out" too? Have you noticed that all your peers who have "given in" regret it? People might act like having sex is what everyone is doing, but deep down they *envy* those who still have their innocence. I caught Kellie Pickler promoting this message on Grand Old Opry last night with her song "Don't You Know You're Beautiful." (You can find a link to the song on the *Nobody Told Me* Facebook fan page.) Praise God that she is using her newfound fame to expose the truth through the cultural lies.

Amber: I loved Kellie on *American Idol* and felt so proud when I heard the song! I haven't been a partier or had sex, and deep down I wondered if it was all it was cracked up to be. This song reminded me that sometimes people act tough on the exterior even though they are filled with regret. Today I am *thankful* that I've chosen to be unique rather than blend in with everyone else!

Comment On This · Love This · Share with Friends

Kylie: My friend had sex at a party while she was drunk. She didn't know what she was doing and regrets the whole thing so much. She hates this guy for taking advantage of her. She can't just take something like this back. She was wondering if this was rape or not.

Comment On This · Love This · Shares with Friends

Pam: Your question is a good one. My best advice is not to drink; alcohol is a *drug,* and taking this drug causes you to lose inhibitions and do things you would never have done without the drug.

This needs to be very clear: Rape is when one person *forces* the other to have sex. The person being attacked clearly says *no* and fights it, but the rapist *forces* it. Force and "taking advantage of" are two different things.

However, if she drank (or used drugs) to the point that she was impaired and no longer capable of giving consent, the law would define it as rape.[2] Hopefully, she went to the emergency room or the authorities to report it.

Comment On This · Love This · Share with Friends

📰 **Newsflash:** Alcohol is a contributing factor in over 75 percent of date rapes.[3]

Pam: You are *not* responsible for what is done *to you!*

Comment On This · Love This · Share with Friends

Sarah: When I was 13, I started dating a family friend's son. He was 17, but we'd known him forever, and he talked about going into the ministry. From outward appearances, he was a good guy. One night after my parents went to bed he started laying me out on the couch, and I screamed, "No!" He apologized and told me that he loved me, and then we agreed to save ourselves for marriage. The next weekend we went to see a movie, only instead of just giving me a goodnight kiss, he forced himself on top of me and assaulted me. I know I don't need to be tested, because I was his first. He really is a good guy. Something must have just come over him. He denies that anything happened. My question is, am I still a virgin?

Comment On This · Love This · Shares with Friends

Pam: I'm so sorry for the pain that you have been through. I am not sure why *anyone* was okay with you "dating" this young man. I don't care if he wants to be a youth pastor. It was completely inappropriate.

A good counselor will not blame you but will help you see where the "warning signs" were and what you could have done differently. This will help you rebuild some of these boundaries and make sure that you do not give in to a "victim mentality" that would put you at risk to be abused again. You seem to have excused him with the "he really is a good guy" comment, and these excuses make me wonder if you really fully understand that your innocence was violated. The law considers you a *child,* and we can't expect children to be able to handle adult situations.

Unfortunately, this young man's behaviors do not indicate the behavior of a novice. For some reason, you are trying to portray this individual as a "good person." His behavior would prove that he is *not*. He is obviously living a lie to the world (by failing to admit what he's done to you), and his bullying of you sexually is a *huge* indication that he has clearly *done this before*. You need to get tested.

This leads me to the virginity question. Virginity is defined by physical activity, not desire. Christ can restore and heal you and empower you to choose "recycled virginity," but it is *not* the same as being a virgin. Here's what I'm getting at. It will be important for you to tell your future spouse about the details of your sexual past. And he will have to have the patience and grace to understand the emotional pain from this violation. *However*, if you do wait for your future spouse, you can still tell him, "I was taken advantage of when I was only 13, but it has been 10 years (or however many years it happens to be for you) since that terrible time, and I have chosen sexual purity for all these years! You are the *first* person that I have *chosen* to have sex with."

Comment On This · Love This · Share with Friends

Newsflash: 85 percent of rapes are committed by someone the rape survivor knows.[4]

💔 Linda's Story

It began when I was about 11 or 12, looking at teen and fashion magazines and comparing the body images of the models to my own body. The perfection I saw on those pages, compared to the image I saw of myself, were devastatingly different. No one will ever be interested in me, I thought, and it haunted my future dreams of finding Mr. Right and living happily ever after.

In seventh grade, one of the most awkward stages of my life, I developed a crush on one of my teachers. He obviously knew of my infatuation, and one day suggested that if I aced his math test, he would give me a kiss! An ugly duckling noticed by an authority figure was unbelievable to me. Of course, I cheated to get the A, he kissed me and things progressed from there. We made out often after school in one of his side rooms, and it made me feel beautiful. This continued through eighth grade as well. A false sense of self-worth began to dominate my thinking and patterned many years of my life to follow.

Another teacher from the same school approached me and wanted to take some "photos" of me because he said that I was beautiful. In high school, a male security guard pulled me out of class one day so that I could perform a "favor" for him. At times I was flattered by the male attention. At other times, I knew that I was being used, because obviously those men had talked with each other. I began to use my looks and charms to play games with the opposite sex but usually ended up being the loser.

Pandora's box of sexual temptations was opened early for me and it caused me a life of difficulty. It made it easier to find the guys who wanted to use me, create more self-doubt and feelings of inferiority, and lead me down the road of finding self-worth through sexual means. If a guy thought I was attractive and wanted me, then I was beautiful. I now know that thinking is false.

God has worked in my life over the years and I have grown and changed. I am worthwhile because He made me and He loves me.

Newsflash: Any sexual contact between a minor and an adult is sexual abuse. If you are or have been abused, please tell a trusted adult *today!*

📝 **Note: Jesus and Sexual Abuse.** Jesus takes sexual abuse seriously. A paraphrased Matthew 18:6 would have Jesus boldly proclaiming, "It would be better that someone had a millstone hung around their neck and be drowned in the sea than have him hurt one of these little ones." I believe He was speaking of all adults who would abuse children sexually or physically! Jesus took this so seriously that He professed that the abuser would be better off dead! Why? Because the reason that sexual abuse and rape are *so horrible* is that the consequences can't just be wiped away. We can't just wave a magic wand and erase the damage. Survivors still need to be tested for STDs, because they could face a lifetime dealing with disease and infertility. And even if they escape physical consequences, the emotional consequences are devastating. *Yes,* there is help and hope in the Lord, but it is a *long, hard* road. To all you brave survivors, know that Christ shares your pain, and justice will be *His!*

Danielle: This reduced me to tears. My mom raised me and never talked to me about sex. I had no concept of healthy boundaries, and I placed myself in situations I had no business being in. My first boyfriend obviously picked up on my lack of boundaries and raped me. I died inside. Because of my Christian faith, I always thought I'd wait until marriage. Anger consumed me—I felt anger toward myself because this happened and toward the boy because of what he had done to me. I felt nasty. To try to bring my life some value again, I desperately searched for someone to love me. Emotionally numb, I started sleeping with every guy willing to make love to me. I wish Christ's love had touched my heart then. My choices only led to more pain.

Comment On This · Love This · Share with Friends

Calista: You are not alone. I, too, was date raped, and in the midst of my depression threw myself out there. In my mind, this was to prove that not all men were violent. A little more than one year later, I found God and became a Christian. My Christian counselor spent time showing me Scriptures of faithful people who had endured hardship, drilling Christ's love for me into my head and ultimately my heart and helping me recognize what godly love looks like in romantic relationships so that I could be strong in the future. Ironically, after I told my next boyfriend about my past, he got mad that I would have willingly had sex with guys after the rape but I wouldn't with him. Needless to say, I dumped him immediately!

Comment On This · Love This · Share with Friends

📰 **Newsflash:** Every two minutes someone is sexually assaulted in the United States.[5]

Jessica: A few months ago, someone sexually assaulted me. I'd known him for years and would have never expected him to do something like this. You hear about this happening, but you never imagine it could happen to you. I wish it was just a bad dream, but this bad dream is my life . . . every day. Is there anything that can help me to move beyond this experience?

Comment On This · Love This · Shares with Friends

Pam: While I would never claim to be an expert on healing the tremendous pain of sexual abuse and rape, here are some practical steps that I think are very important:

1. **Find a qualified counselor**—This cannot be over-emphasized. A common mistake sex abuse survivors make is that they will be able to heal and get through it on their own. Let a Christian professional help you work through your emotions and heal in the proper steps.

2. **Tell someone you love**—Keeping a secret of this magnitude can make you a victim again! You are further victimized because you are holding your emotions, pain and fear inside. Help free yourself by talking to someone you trust.

3. **Search for a good support group**—You are not alone, and you could gain from a shared experience with others. The only word of caution is to make sure you get a good group leader. The one potential negative with groups is to wallow in the pain and stay there rather than discuss the experiences and help each other move forward.

4. **Journal your progress**—Initially, you might find that many things trigger pain. Over time your heart will begin to heal and you will be able to handle those situations. If you journal what you were able to do, and focus on the positive, you can look back at that journal on a rough day and see how far you've come.

5. **Dig into God's Word**—Sometimes when life is painful, people have a tendency to push God away rather than pull Him in. This leaves them no option but to survive on their own strength, and it perpetuates the pain. Hear what God has to say. Be reminded of His love.

Comment On This · Love This · Share with Friends

📰 **Newsflash:** If you have had sex by choice or because something was done to you, *help is available*. Please call 1-800-395-HELP and your local pregnancy care center will meet with you for counsel as well as provide names of additional community resources.

 Pam: "'For I know the plans I have for you,' declares the LORD, 'plans to prosper you and not to harm you, plans to give you hope and a future'" (Jeremiah 29:11).

Comment On This · Love This · Shares with Friends

SECTION TWO:

The Price Paid

Chapter 4

Math Meets Sex Ed: 1 Plus 1 Equals 3

 Pam: Here are some common thoughts and feelings I heard from my days at the Pregnancy center: "This can't be happening to me. Why haven't I gotten my period? We were being "safe." Am I under too much stress? Did I exercise too much? Am I just irregular? I feel like I could vomit. I don't want to be sitting in this pregnancy center on this tiny couch waiting for this result. Why me?!"

Comment On This · Love This · Shares with Friends

 Monica: I can totally relate. I'm sitting here in shock. My boyfriend and I have been together for a year. A couple of months ago we thought we'd take our relationship to the next level and started having sex. Well, my period was a couple of days late, so I bought a pregnancy test on the way home from school and took it before my parents got home. There were two lines. I'm pregnant. I've been hiding in my room, crying, all afternoon. What am I going to do? How did having sex result in such a horrible feeling? I'm going to have to tell my boyfriend and my parents . . . and they will all be upset. Please help me.

Comment On This · Love This · Share with Friends

 Pam: I'm so sorry, Monica. Discovering that you are pregnant is understandably very scary; and figuring out how you are going to talk with the people around you can feel overwhelming. Before you get ahead of yourself, it is important that you take some time to take a deep breath and think this through. Remember, the people that love you are not against you. They will want to be helpful.

If your boyfriend is having sex with you, he has to know that pregnancy is a possibility. Tell him that you were "late," so you took a pregnancy test and it was positive. Then, take time to listen to him and make a call to your nearby pregnancy care center for an appointment together. Once at the center, they will confirm the pregnancy and provide information about pregnancy options with *both* of you. This is *critical*, because your boyfriend's input will impact your decision, and it's important for him to fully understand the ramifications of all the possible choices you face for your baby, your health and your future.

When it comes to talking with your parents, there is no one-size-fits-all perfect approach to telling them. Different relationships, different temperaments and different beliefs could affect the wording you use or where you choose to tell them. If you have any questions about that, please talk to the pregnancy care center counselor about it. They can talk in depth with you about the relationship you share with your parents and give you suggestions and resources that will best help you approach them. Regardless, it probably isn't going to be easy. Simply sitting down, looking them in the eye and sharing your heart is the best thing you can do.

Monica, as you work through your questions and emotions, it is important that you take your time. Please *do not* make any snap decisions. Remember, you and your boyfriend have to live with whatever choice you make for the rest of your life.

Comment On This · Love This · Share with Friends

📰 **Newsflash:** One out of every three females in the United States gets pregnant before the age of 20.[1]

☞ **Note: No Easy Way Out.** Panic overwhelms girls when they find out they are pregnant and didn't plan to be. Throughout my years of counseling in the pregnancy care center, I watched hundreds of girls look at their positive test result and immediately want an easy, painless way out of the situation only to find out that there isn't one. In reality, a girl's choices are bad, terrible and even worse.

There is *no* easy way out of a pregnancy you didn't plan. If you or someone you know is pregnant and didn't intend to be, please seek help at a local pregnancy care center (this toll-free number will help you find the center near you: 1-800-395-HELP) and *take time* to pray over your options. I know it is tough, but you had a good choice. That was before you chose to have sex. Now *every* option will carry painful, lifelong consequences.

Pam: Ending a human life will never end your human suffering.

Comment On This · Love This · Shares with Friends

Ann: So true. I had an abortion, and no one knows except the father of the baby. I really thought it was the perfect "solution" at the time, but not a day goes by that I don't think about my baby. When I see children the age mine would have been, I cry. I desperately wish I could take it back.

Comment On This · Love This · Share with Friends

Thea: I also thought it would make things better compared to how I was feeling before, but I was totally wrong. I am in so much pain, and there is nothing anyone can do about it. This sucks.

Comment On This · Love This · Share with Friends

Kane: My girlfriend had an abortion and didn't tell me until after she did it. I never got a say. I never got a voice. I will never have sex again until I'm married, because I could not bear hearing, "I aborted your baby" ever again.

Comment On This · Love This · Share with Friends

Pam: Your comments are sobering. While society paints a rosy picture that abortion is a trouble-free, easy, quick solution, your stories reiterate the truth. Abortion is painful and has lifelong consequences. Post-abortive women and men are still in counseling 5, 10, 15 years later, with failed relationships, suicidal thoughts, eating disorders, depression, cutting, and the list goes on. You can't take back an abortion. It is not like going to the dentist to get your tooth pulled. I pray for healing for all of you who are silently suffering. And I pray that those facing an unplanned pregnancy will listen to the wisdom in the pain of those who have walked this road before them.

Comment On This · Love This · Share with Friends

📰 **Newsflash:** Not all facilities explain every physical, emotional and spiritual risk that can follow an abortion experience, nor do they all explain and show fetal development in pre-abortion counseling. In fact, one survey of American women found that 84 percent didn't feel they had received adequate counseling prior to their abortion.[2] This lack of information hurts mothers and fathers and costs babies their lives.

Trina: Can my parents force me to have an abortion if I'm not legally an adult?

Comment On This · Love This · Shares with Friends

Pam: No. It is illegal for anyone to force you to have an abortion. Likewise, it is illegal for anyone to do the abortion if you get to the facility and change your mind there. It is your *right* to say no, even if you are a minor being pressured by your parents.

Please get this, because it is very important. Your life may feel miserable if the people around you are insisting that you have an abortion. But *you* have to live with this, and *you* get the final say. So, if you are not comfortable with it and you are not safe at home or in your relationship, please get to your local pregnancy care center and they will have names of safe places for you to go.

Comment On This · Love This · Share with Friends

💔 Theo's Story

My life could easily have been yours . . . just a simple American family. I aspired to play baseball and went to church on the holidays.

In 2006, I found out my girlfriend was pregnant. Neither of us planned this pregnancy or had even talked about the possibility of getting pregnant. That was about to become my biggest regret.

I brought her to a pregnancy care center so that she could explore her options other than having an abortion. At eight weeks, we had an ultrasound. Our child had fingers, toes, eyes, everything. I saw and heard my child's heart beat, and I cried. It was a very overwhelming and beautiful experience for me. My girlfriend insisted she was going to have an abortion that weekend and broke up with me.

I called the abortion clinic and asked what my rights were; they said, "You don't have any, and don't call back." They told me that it wasn't a child, it was a fetus, and to never call again or they would involve the police, and if I showed up on Saturday to try to stop my girlfriend from having an abortion, they would have me arrested. My hands were tied. I, as a father, had no legal right to protect my child from a death committed by a doctor. I called everyone imaginable to see what my rights were, and I got the same answer: No rights.

The week before my child was aborted, I went to try one more time to ask the mother of my child to not do this, but she was adamant about having an abortion and told me to leave. So I asked her if I could do one last thing before I left. She told me that was fine. I then got on my knees and kissed the stomach of the mother of my child and said, "I love you, and Daddy will see you in heaven." Then I took the ultrasound pictures and left.

The day my child was aborted was a very painful day for me. I was informed that my child had been aborted in the afternoon on December 2, 2006. It was the most painful experience I have ever been through. My relationship ended with the woman that I thought I was going to marry, and I lost my first child. I didn't want to go on; I was in too much pain. I didn't eat. I didn't sleep. I had nightmares of my child being aborted. The day after the abortion, I went to see my pastor, and he suggested that I have a memorial for my unborn child. I took his advice and had one the following Sunday at his church. I had my parents and a few friends come. It was a short ceremony, but very painful. I never thought that my child would meet God before I did.

After that day, things were still very painful. I still couldn't sleep or eat, and thoughts of suicide filled my head every waking hour. I joined Bible studies and post-abortion Bible studies as much as possible. I miss my baby every single day. I know my child is now in the arms of Jesus, and one day, I will meet him and hold him in heaven.

Anthony: My girlfriend is pregnant and, despite the things I read, I want her to have an abortion. If she carries this baby, it will be an embarrassment to me. I can't have that. What do I do?

Comment On This · Love This · Shares with Friends

 Pam: You are in a very precarious situation. Despite your first instinct to hit the pavement running as fast and as far from the situation as possible, please *do not* do that! This is the time to man up. Never will you have a moment as critical as this. I've got news for you. Back when you were being "manly" and messing around, you were not. There is nothing "manly" about sex. After all, it takes no talent or ability. Anyone can have sex. My dog can have sex. But it takes character to own up to the unexpected outcomes. It takes character to look that young lady in the eye who is desperately wanting to take back all those past decisions just as badly as you and say, "I am here. I'm not going to desert you. I will be a part of this." Remember, you were 50 percent of this equation, and running will not pretend it away. Be wise!

Comment On This · Love This · Share with Friends

@ **Link:** For anyone who thinks that abortion would be a convenient choice, please read these powerful words by Mary Cate Bratcher (http://www.renewamerica.com/columns/abbott/100111).

Death for My Convenience
I was in college
And thought I was grown.
I felt like a big shot
Doing whatever I wanted living on my own.

I was into the campus party life,
Throwing caution to the wind.
My boyfriend and I played house
Like we were husband and wife.

Before I knew it, I was pregnant with child.
I lied to myself
And went into denial.
I thought of my baby as a blob.

My sister paid for my abortion.
Mother could not find out.
All I wanted was my degree
And do whatever I darn well pleased.

I almost bled to death after the abortion procedure.
I was in physical pain
And never thought about what I had done
to my little son!

My boyfriend dumped me,
I married someone else.
I began to drink, curse and act wild.
I never knew it had to do with what I did to my child.

I went to the hospital
Countless times for attempted suicide.
I wanted to die.
I'd lived a lie.

One night I fell on my knees.
I begged God, "Please forgive me."
I realized my abortion was my choice.
My baby boy had no voice.

My baby's fate was doomed
By having him torn apart
And ripped right out of my womb.
I had chosen his death for my convenience.

(In Loving Memory of Sarra's Baby)[3]

Pam: Society may glamorize teen pregnancy, but there is nothing glamorous about being a teen parent!
Comment On This · Love This · Share with Friends

Ali: Isn't that the truth! Teen pregnancy has become so accepted, and the media even shows programs like "The Pregnancy Pact" where teens are trying to get pregnant. It makes me sad. I have a toddler, and I'm stressed every day. I'm trying to finish school and work a part-time job to help support him. His dad left. I always dreamed of having a family but never wanted it to look like this.
Comment On This · Love This · Share with Friends

📰 **Newsflash:** Less than one-third of teens who begin their families before age 18 ever earn a high school diploma, and only 1.5 percent earn a college degree by age 30.[4] Unfortunately, the child has a 64 percent chance of growing up in poverty.[5]

💜 Heather's Story

My story began my junior year of high school. Around Christmas time, I found out that I was pregnant. My boyfriend who was the father and I had been dating approximately one year. I was scared beyond words—scared about having a child, scared about telling my parents, scared for what this would mean for me and for the future.

Abortion was never an option for me. I did meet with an adoption counselor, but it wasn't the right choice for me. I felt I had a good enough support system to take care of a child, myself and still be able to attend school. Telling my parents I was pregnant was one of the hardest things I have ever had to do. I was completely and totally ashamed. The words "I am pregnant" never even left my mouth. While trying to choke back sobs, I simply stated I had missed my period. My mom was able to figure out what this meant and she then told my father nearly immediately. They both started crying. I will never forget that day. I knew they were so disappointed in me, and I was disappointed in myself. I was never able to speak the words to my friends either, but over time they figured it out.

Both my family and my boyfriend were incredibly supportive throughout my pregnancy. Of course, I naturally thought that I would be with the father of my child forever. Not only did I think that before I got pregnant, but after I found out I was pregnant this feeling intensified, as I wanted to make it work for the baby.

On September 2, 1998, my baby girl, Katelyn, entered this world. Even though the circumstances of her birth were not ideal, having her enter my life was a happy day.

When Katelyn was a toddler, my faith blossomed to a living faith. At about that time, my feelings for Katelyn's father started to change and eventually I knew that it wouldn't work out for us to be together. The feeling was hard for me to come to terms with. I remember crying, thinking, *I don't want this for my daughter,* and *Who is ever going to want to date someone my age with a child? Who would even want me?* Later, my doctor said, "If a person wouldn't want to be with you because of your daughter, then they are not the kind of person you would want to be with anyhow." That never left me. In many ways it gave me hope.

Shortly thereafter, I met my future husband—an extremely loving, godly man who I believe was put on this earth for me. He was and still is so good to Katelyn and me. We now have three other children together.

Even though my story is a success in that I finished school and married a wonderful man, the decision to have sex and then ultimately get pregnant is something that will never leave me. I believe that sexual sin is one of the most powerful sins and it is a sin that can stay with you for a lifetime. Although there isn't one day I am not thankful for my daughter, and I consider it a blessing to be a part of her life, I wish I would've made a different choice.

The shame of that pregnancy is something I carry with me to this day. I am not sure it will ever leave me. I still worry about what people might think of me if they knew I was a "teen mom." Would they not want their child to be friends with my daughter? Do they not want their child around me? I hate having to share holidays with the father of my daughter. I feel sick when she goes to her dad's house on the weekend; it is actually something I don't even like to think about. It is especially difficult knowing he has a different set of values and parents differently than I do. That is not to say I do not get along with my daughter's father, because I do and always will for the sake of our daughter. It is just difficult, and I believe it always will be.

I try not to look ahead too much to the future and what struggles it might bring, as worry is never good, and I have to trust in a sovereign God. Although there will always be struggles that will go along with having a child as a teenager, I am continually reminded that we serve a God who is faithful and who loves me and my daughter more than we can even imagine. I know that He will always provide, and He is there to see me through the struggles, knowing that He will never give me anything more than we can handle together. I trust Him and take one day at a time.

Joe: My girlfriend is pregnant and she says it's my baby. I'm not even sure it's really mine. What if it's not? Am I going to be expected to pay for this kid if she decides to keep it, because that's what she says she's doing? I don't want her to, and if she goes against my wishes for the pregnancy, I shouldn't have to pay.

Comment On This · Love This · Shares with Friends

Pam: Joe, *pregnancy doesn't just affect females*. It affects mom, dad and baby. Unfortunately for you, dads have absolutely *no rights*. Your girlfriend can do with your child, your flesh and blood, whatever she wants. And, suing her for stealing your sperm might prove a bit difficult! This is why it is important to think before you have sex!

I would encourage you to get a paternity test. Should you be named the baby's father, your decision to have sex will become directly linked to your checkbook.

Quite frankly, children are expensive. Because that is true, the United States Administration for Children and Families Office of Public Affairs is trying to decrease the general public's need to foot the bill for unmarried people's irresponsible choices.

And, if your gut response is to flee, think again. If paternity is not voluntarily admitted, the court can serve you papers requiring you to show up for blood testing. Because this is a federal initiative, it does not matter if you are in a different state or some small community, you will be found.

Once you are officially "daddy," you will be expected to pony up the dough needed for that child to thrive. If you don't willingly send the amount the court has determined, the government will seek you out. They will withhold your income, and that check that you are getting from Burger King or Wal-Mart will suddenly be next to nothing. In our country, over 69 percent of child support is paid this way.[6]

If your payment is past due, the fines will be much steeper than when you forget to return your library book. The most immediate impact could come through driver's license suspension. Your financial accounts could be frozen and passport denied. Furthermore, information may be reported to credit bureaus and you will struggle to get that new car, credit card or home when you want it. Some states will even take criminal action against you.

While some states have responded differently to the laws, all states must respond to the federal laws to receive funding, so they will be doing everything within their power to collect child support. This is serious, Joe.

Aside from the law, you made a CHOICE to sleep with this girl and you can't tell me that you didn't know pregnancy was a possibility. You *cannot possibly* have sex under *any circumstance* and think that there is no risk. There is always risk. Now a baby is on the way. You need to step up to the plate.

I'm thankful that neither of you questioned giving this baby life. The next step is to determine whose home this precious child will grow up in—hers or with adoptive parents. Although you can't make that choice, you can urge her to at least speak with an adoption counselor. Your local pregnancy care center can set up a free consultation and provide you both with information on all of today's adoption options.

Comment On This · Love This · Share with Friends

📰 **Newsflash:** Teen marriage: 8 out of 10 teenage fathers do not marry the mother of their first child.[7]

 Pam: Adoption is the ability of the young girl to take the child she has carried for nine months and loves with everything that she is and to say, "I want the best for you, and I am not it. And, I'm willing to go through this pain to give you, my child, a family." It takes a lot of courage, a lot of maturity and a lot of love.

Comment On This · Love This · Shares with Friends

 Marlie: I'm pregnant. I'm due very soon, and I love him; but, as stated in your update, I know I'm not the best for him. I want him to have a family, with a mom and dad and maybe a family pet. I can't give him those things. I mean, I'm just learning geometry and wasn't supposed to be dating in the first place. I'm really considering adoption. Or, will no one want him because he's from a teen? I just want what is best for him.

Comment On This · Love This · Share with Friends

Pam: I commend you for loving this child enough to give him life. First, let me say that there is *no child* that would not be wanted or loved by someone. Adoption fulfills another person's dream. Marvelously and magnificently, these children have been doubly loved by birth parents who chose life and made plans that were in the child's best interest *and* by adoptive parents who have long prayed to become a mom and dad.

That said, you have to do for this child what is best for you in your situation. From my own experience, I know that adoption is a true act of love. If my birth mom had kept me, I would not have had the opportunities that I did growing up. I was fortunate enough to be in a Christian home with a financially stable mom and dad who loved each other and us very much. They were always present and doing what they could to guide us and give us the best. I'm so thankful to my birth mom and adoptive parents for that gift.

To further explore your adoption options, please call your pregnancy care center. Through consultations with adoption counselors/attorneys, you can learn more about varying adoption plans and have all your questions answered free of charge. With that information, you can pray for wisdom and strength as you make your final decision.

Comment On This · Love This · Share with Friends

📝 **Note: Pam's Story.** Forty-six years ago in Michigan, a young woman became pregnant. She had a lot of difficult choices to make, maybe more so than some, because she was raped. Abortion may have been legal in Michigan, in the case of rape in the 1960s, but this 15-year-old girl chose to give her child life and then place that child with an adoptive family. That child was me.

My biological father is a rapist. I don't even know my ethnicity, but my life still has value, and it isn't worth any less than yours just because of how I was conceived. And I do not believe that I deserved the death penalty because of the crime of my father. All of my life I have had to listen to the rhetoric that every child should be wanted and planned. I have heard people say, "I wouldn't have an abortion, that would be terrible; but if it were rape, well then . . ." I guess that means that I am a "mistake"! Well, I don't believe that. I believe that every child is wanted by someone and that God in His mercy had a plan for me.

I've asked all the tough questions: Did God plan me? Does God plan rape? I memorized Scripture verses when I was little, like, "You loved me before the creation of the world" (John 17:24) and "Before I formed you in the womb I knew you" (Jeremiah 1:5). Did that mean me? I might not have all the answers to those difficult questions, but this is what I do know: I know that my God is so awesome and so amazing that He is capable of taking our worst pain, whether it was something that we chose or whether it was something that was done to us, and my God can make something very beautiful come from that. That is the amazing grace of God—His ability to take even what Satan meant for evil and make something good come from it.

Please do not think for a moment that I would ever stand before anyone and justify rape by my existence. My existence does not justify rape. Never. Rape is still wrong. Rape is still a horrifying violation of another human being. What we can say very clearly is that the behavior was wrong but the child is a gift from God, created in His image.

I've not met my birth mom, but if I get that chance, I'm going to wrap my arms around her and tell her that I love her, because she loved me. She loved me enough to give me my life, and then she loved me enough to give me the next most special gift that I was ever given—my family. I am eternally grateful for her selfless act of love.

Newsflash: Adopted teenagers are as emotionally stable as non-adopted teenagers.[8]

Renae: I am three months pregnant. The baby's father and I have decided that we think it would be best to place our baby for adoption. The problem is that my parents don't know that I'm considering adoption, and I don't know how to tell them. After all, this baby is a part of their family too. I'm so stressed.

Comment On This · Love This · Shares with Friends

Pam: I admire you. The fact that you and your boyfriend have discussed this difficult issue and that you both genuinely recognize what you are not yet ready for parenting shows extreme maturity.

Please remember that at this point you are *projecting* how your parents will respond. I'm sure that finding out you were pregnant was challenging for them, and the fact that they have embraced your situation with grace shows godly love. *But*, that doesn't mean they are happy about it. As a parent, I can assure you that they want the best for you. Support does not equal an expectation that you will parent this baby. I'd suggest family therapy with a Christian counselor so that you can process your experience together. This will help to keep your communication flowing and bring you closer together in the process.

If you feel pressured to keep the baby and do not feel ready, please remember that this is *your choice*. You might be young, but you still get to make the decision. The reality is that you cannot keep your baby out of fear of disappointing someone else. This decision *is* going to change your life . . . either because your "I love you" meant saying a difficult goodbye or because your life is transformed from high school games and going to movies with your friends into changing diapers, feeding your infant and making yourself available to meet the needs of your child.

Guilt should *never* motivate your decision. Prayer *should*. Listen to God and you'll do what is right for you.

Comment On This · Love This · Share with Friends

🐾 Denae's Story

A month after I turned 16, I became pregnant by my boyfriend of two years who was also 16. I was raised in a Christian home and I knew that sex before marriage was wrong. I didn't believe in abortion, so that was never an option for me. I ended up having to move into a maternity home because the situation with my boyfriend was getting out of control.

My daughter was born in May 2003. Two days after her birth, I did the hardest thing I'll probably ever have to do. I handed my precious little girl to her adoptive mother in the hospital parking lot. I wept for months over the "loss" of my child, even though I knew it was the best for my baby.

God is helping me overcome a lot of my grief. I chose open adoption, so I get to see my baby several times a year, and her adoptive mother sends me emails and pictures weekly to keep me updated. My baby will grow up knowing that I'm her birth mommy and that I chose her family especially for her. My child will always know how much I loved her and that she was adopted because of that love.

I wanted my daughter to have a shot at life with a stable Christian family. Many people think that a birth mother who releases her child for adoption does not love or want that child. This angers me so much because there is nothing I love more than my baby, and I wanted badly to parent her. But, I had to make the responsible choice for my baby because her future depended on me. It is so heartbreaking to get comments from people like, "How could you give your baby away?" They don't understand that I didn't "give her away." I gave her a chance.

Pam: "The answer to a crisis pregnancy is to eliminate the crisis, not the child" (Frederica Mathewes-Green).

Comment On This · Love This · Shares with Friends

Chapter 5

STDs:
The Gift that Keeps on Giving

Pam: While there is a lot of emphasis on HIV/AIDS, most students do not understand the risk of sexually transmitted disease, how many different diseases are out there and how many of their friends are infected. You can't tell if someone is infected just by looking at him or her and a person usually won't share that bit of information with even his or her closest friends. Your chance of being infected with an STD is far greater than your risk of becoming pregnant!

Comment On This · Love This · Shares with Friends

Cody: Far higher? Are you sure? I don't know anyone in my class that has an STD, but I could specifically name the girls that are pregnant.

Comment On This · Love This · Share with Friends

Pam: Cody, your classmates' pregnancies might eventually become obvious, but STDs will *not*. And your friends typically won't announce these diagnoses to the world. You aren't going to walk into homeroom and hear, "Hey, guys, I went to the doctor yesterday and found out that I have herpes. Please make sure the whole school knows by the end of the day." Students, *if* they know they are infected, typically keep this quiet!

Comment On This · Love This · Share with Friends

Dave: I saw your status update and I want numbers. How many people really have an STD? It can't be that many.

Comment On This · Love This · Shares with Friends

Pam: *Au contraire*, Dave! Here is the stat—1 in 4 teens are infected with at least one STD.[1] That's right, 1 in 4. Next time you are sitting in class, count every fourth person. Sobering, isn't it? For the virgins, which are approximately half of you, there is no need to worry, because there is *no risk*. But for those that are sexually active, that means that you have about a 50/50 chance of being infected at any given time. Just something to think about!

Comment On This · Love This · Share with Friends

Newsflash: STDs are the most common diseases in America next to the common cold and flu.[2]

 April: Before hearing your talk, I never knew there were so many STDs. But, what if you only sleep with people that are virgins? Then you can't get a disease, right?

Comment On This · Love This · Shares with Friends

 Pam: I have a couple of issues with this. First of all, why would you *want* to sleep with multiple people? This indicates a longing for love and attention that is not being met in your life, but you *will not* find it through sex. Let's be realistic. These boys don't care about you! They care about what you are giving them.

Second, what makes you think that these people are truly virgins who have not crossed the line for STDs? That assumes that they can be trusted. If they know that you are *interested* in having sex with them, do you really think they are going to "honestly" share their sexual history with you, sharing every detail? Of course not! They most likely believe that if they tell you they are not virgins, you would choose to not have sex with them, so it is better to lie in order to get what they want. There is no real way that you can know if someone is a virgin; you haven't been with them every second of their life!

Furthermore, it *does not* take "penetrative sex" to get an STD. Did you get that? Many will claim, "Yes, I'm a virgin," only counting vaginal intercourse as sex. WRONG! The Medical Institute for Sexual Health (MISH) states, "Sex occurs when one person touches another person's genitals and causes that person to get sexually excited."[3] Did you get that? The medical community defines sex as any genital contact. This means that hand to genital contact, and vaginal, anal and oral sex are all classified as sex and place you at risk for STDs. *Anyone* who has engaged in that activity *needs* to be tested and should not be considered a "safe" partner.

Comment On This · Love This · Share with Friends

@ **Link:** How many people have you been exposed to?[4] (http://www.teens4pure energy.com/teens4/chart.htm) Check out the sexual exposure chart on the *Nobody Told Me* Facebook fan page.

🖉 **Note: Sexually transmitted diseases are not equal opportunity destroyers.** Girls will pay a *higher* price *physically* every time! Sorry, girls, I know this doesn't seem fair, but if you haven't been told yet, LIFE ISN'T FAIR. In case you missed this important point during your fifth grade "talk" with boys in one room and girls in the other, *we're different!* Boys' and girls' bodies are *not* the same. Women are easier to infect and easier to damage.

And because you are developing, and your body is changing, you are at an even higher risk than you will be when you are older. Females have a "risk zone," medically referred to as "ectopy," that exposes cells "highly susceptible to STIs" and cervical cancers.[5] While this "risk zone" shrinks as women mature, it is largest in adolescent girls, meaning *you* are at an even *higher* risk for infections that could leave you scarred, damaged, infertile or worse yet, dead. Protect your future! WAIT!

Newsflash: Today, in the next 24 hours, more than 10,000 teens will find out that they have an STD.[6]

 Clay: I read your post and it has me thinking about my girlfriend. We have sex, and I want to try and protect her. A lot of times we use condoms, but maybe she should get on birth control or something too. Would that help?
Comment On This · Love This · Shares with Friends

 Pam: The *only* way that you can protect your girlfriend is by avoiding *all* genital contact.

It astounds me that people are willing to stake their future on a tiny piece of latex. Did you know that condoms fail in preventing pregnancy 15 percent of the time?[7] That means that more than one in six people trying to prevent pregnancy this year will find out that a baby is on the way. When it comes to STDs, condoms reduce the risk, at best, from *some* diseases, and there is virtually no evidence that they will prevent the transmission of diseases like HPV and herpes, because they are transmitted by "skin" contact, not necessarily bodily fluid, anywhere in the entire genital area, which is much larger than the region covered by the condom. The bottom line is that condoms fail and fail often. Is it really worth the risk?

I'm glad that you asked about birth control, because you clearly do not understand its purpose. Birth control was designed to prevent pregnancy, not to keep you from being infected with an STD. In fact, studies have confirmed that hormonal birth control *increases* the risk of contracting a disease.[8] Already at higher risk because of her age, your girlfriend's risk could be exacerbated with hormonal birth control. That cervical "risk zone" discussed in the note is made even larger from elements in hormonal birth control. Not good. The progesterone could suppress her immune system, thin the lining of her uterus and change her monthly bleeding, causing additional opportunity for those STDs to infect her!

If you genuinely care about this girl, set a new standard: *no genital contact* until marriage. Not only will that eliminate her risk for disease, but it will also protect her heart and your relationship and your future wife (just in case it does not happen to be her, which statistically is a good bet)!

Comment On This · Love This · Share with Friends

💔 Haily's Story

I always believed in saving sex for marriage, and yet I have joined the ranks of gullible girls who caved in to the first guy who said, "What we have is special."

Unbeknownst to me, he had gonorrhea. I got infected and had to be treated. I thought that was bad enough. But, at my yearly pap, the doctor found abnormal cells and had to start treatments for HPV. Suddenly, I'd gone from a "pure girl" to one infected with multiple STDs.

I spend many nights crying. Any time a guy acts interested in me, I act cold to turn him away. My best friend tries to reassure me that there is someone out there who will love and accept me regardless of my health history; but who really wants to be with someone infected with a disease if they've lived their life making right choices?

I'm so frustrated with myself.

Pam: You cannot cure or treat a disease you do not know that you have. Many, if not most, infected students are completely unaware they are infected!

Comment On This · Love This · Shares with Friends

Laura: Is there medicine for every kind of STD?

Comment On This · Love This · Share with Friends

Pam: While there are medications to treat symptoms of STDs, not all can be cured. You see, there are two types of STDs, bacterial and viral. A bacterial infection is curable. There is medication that can rid your body of the disease. A virus, on the other hand, is not. If you get a virus, it is for life. There might be medications to treat the symptoms of these STDs (although some may lay dormant and you may feel asymptomatic), but that is not the same as a cure.

Comment On This · Love This · Share with Friends

@ **Link:** Have you been tested for these things? STDs are serious diseases with serious consequences. *Never* assume that you are "safe." If you have any form of genital contact, you need to get tested as soon as possible![9] (http://www.medinstitute.org/public/121.cfm)

1. bacterial vaginosis
2. chancroid
3. chlamydia
4. donovanosis
5. gonorrhea
6. lymphogranuloma venereum
7. mycoplasma, genital
8. syphilis
9. treponematosis, endemic
10. lice, pubic
11. scabies
12. candidiasis, vulvovaginal
13. amebiasis
14. cryptosporidium
15. giardiasis
16. trichomoniasis
17. cytomegalovirus
18. Epstein Barr virus
19. hepatitis A
20. hepatitis B
21. hepatitis C
22. hepaptitis D
23. herpes simplex virus (HSV-1 and HSV-2)
24. human immunodeficiency virus (HIV)
25. human papillomavirus (HPV)
26. human T-cell lymphotropic virus (HTLV-1)
27. molluscum contagiosum

Pam: I'm going to post some snapshot information of STDs here. Follow along to get up-to-date information!

Comment On This · Love This · Shares with Friends

Snapshot: Chlamydia

Nickname: The Silent Disease

Category: Bacteria

Number Infected: 1,030,911 chlamydial infections were reported to CDC from 50 states and the District of Columbia in 2006.[10]

How it is spread: Vaginal, anal and oral sex, as well as from mother to baby in childbirth.

What's the big deal: Most people who carry Chlamydia have no idea that they are infected. For women, this causes damage of the reproductive organs and leads to pelvic inflammatory disease (PID) and subsequent infertility. An astonishingly high 40 percent of women with untreated Chlamydia will develop PID.[11] New medical data also indicates that even women who receive treatment may suffer years down the road. We now know that while Chlamydia is hiding out in the cells it makes a protein called HSP. Dr. Grossman explains, "The HSP was released when the cell died. Her white cells, on the patrol for alien matter, correctly identified the HSP as foreign, and made antibodies. In the process, the white cells memorized the architecture of the HSP."[12] That is all great when you're fighting Chlamydia, but years down the road when you want to get pregnant you might have difficulty because one of the first proteins that baby will make is HSP. Your body will remember this from when you had the chlamydia infection and come fighting once more—only this time it will result in the potential loss of the baby you so badly wanted. Long-term complications for men are far less frequent, although in some the infection may migrate to the epididymis and cause sterility. Both males and females are at risk for developing Reiter's syndrome, which is arthritis along with skin lesions and inflamed eyes and urethra.

Alicia: I want to know if it's possible to cure Chlamydia with an over-the-counter cream for vaginal infections. If I ask my mom to fill the prescription she will know that I'm infected.
Comment On This · Love This · Share with Friends

Pam: An over-the-counter cream is not the same and will not cure the infection. Among the bacterial STDs, Chlamydia is one of the most prevalent. Unfortunately, this is a disease on the rise, particularly among teenagers. In fact, the American Medical Association has stated that all girls between the ages of 12 and 19 who have had sex should be tested every six months.[13] Because it is a bacteria, one round of antibiotics should wipe this out, but you need to be tested, and anyone testing positive *needs* to fill and take the medication as prescribed by your doctor.
Comment On This · Love This · Share with Friends

Snapshot: Gonorrhea

Nickname: The clap

Category: Bacteria

Number Infected: More than 700,000 cases in the United States[14]

How it is spread: Contact with infected penis, vagina, mouth or anus. It can also be spread from mother to child in childbirth.

What's the big deal: For females, PID, which increases your risk for infertility and ectopic pregnancy, is a real danger. Males, you are once again at risk for epididymitis. Both males and females infected with gonorrhea have increased potential to acquire HIV[15] and even possible death, as this disease can spread to the blood and joints.

Pam: Like Chlamydia, gonorrhea requires prescription antibiotics for treatment. However, gonorrhea has become more resistant to antibiotics over the years.[16] This is particularly frightening, considering (1) the severity of the consequences, and (2) teenagers have the highest rate of infection, increasing their potential for damage before childbearing years.[17]

Comment On This · Love This · Shares with Friends

📰 **Newsflash:** 15 percent of all infertile American women are infertile because of tubal damage caused by an STD.[18]

💬 Tonya's Story

Recently, I started experiencing some terrible stomachaches. I assumed that it was a simple stomach bug that I could just visit the physician and get some medicine for.

I walked out shocked. When she pushed on my ovaries, I felt terrible shooting pains. I shot up on the bed and curled over in pain. You would not believe how bad it hurt. Because of my response, she did a gynecological exam and told me that my cervix was red and bloody. I couldn't believe it.

My simple trip to the doctor turned into an emotional nightmare. I have gonorrhea. I have an STD! Never in a million years did I think this could happen to me.

Snapshot: Human Immunodeficiency Virus/Acquired Immunodeficiency Virus

Nickname: HIV/AIDS

Category: Virus

Number Infected: 1.2 million[19]

How it is spread: Vaginal, anal and oral sex with an infected partner. It is also spread from sharing infected needles and from mother to child.

What's the big deal? There is no cure for AIDS. While there are antiviral medications to prolong life, people with this disease have a death sentence.

Maliya: I heard that you can get HIV from French kissing. Is that true?

Comment On This · Love This · Share with Friends

Pam: There is an informational website about the CDC from Albany University that states, "Kissing generally does not present a risk, but because of the theoretical risk of HIV transmission through blood that might be present in the mouth, CDC does not recommend engaging in deep (French) kissing with an infected person, or person whose infection status is unknown."[20]

Herpes simplex virus 1 (HSV1), seen as cold sores on the mouth, is very contagious through kissing.

This reminds us that kissing IS intimate. Does it mean that you should always be fearful? No. But it does mean that you need to *be careful* about who you are kissing. It shouldn't be "just anyone." It should be someone that you could see yourself with long term. Protect your health and your heart.

Comment On This · Love This · Share with Friends

Newsflash: Each year there are 40,000 new HIV infections in the United States, and yet 25 percent of infected individuals do not know they have it.[21]

Snapshot: Human Papillomavirus (HPV)

Nickname: Genital Warts

Category: Virus

Number Infected: Approximately 20 million American's are currently infected[22]

How it is spread: Through any genital contact with an infected partner. It is also possible for a pregnant mother to pass the disease to her newborn during vaginal delivery.

What's the big deal: Girls pay a much higher price for this disease. According to the National Cancer Institute, HPV is the major cause of cervical cancer today. In our society, more than 1 in 2 sexually active singles will contract this disease.[23] On a much smaller scale, it is also linked with cancer of the vulva, vagina, penis, anus and throat.

Christa: I've had sex with four different guys, and until you spoke I didn't realize all the risks. When you were talking about HPV I got really scared because the third guy I slept with wasn't a virgin. We did use a condom but you said that HPV could still be passed on because of the skin-to-skin contact thing. I was confused about how my boyfriend and I get tested for this disease.

Comment On This · Love This · Share with Friends

Pam: I am thankful that you are getting tested. To screen for HPV, physicians most frequently do routine pap smears to detect the presence of abnormal cervical cells. If that comes back abnormal, many doctors will continue on with a specific HPV test to more specifically detect the presence of HPV.

As far as your boyfriend goes, they *do not currently test males* for HPV. Obviously boys are carriers and pass it on, but unless they present with genital warts, which actually exist in only a very small percent of cases, you *will not know*. This is why any guy that has had genital contact prior to marriage *needs* to tell his future spouse because she will need to get regular pap smears. It also means that *no girl* can trust a guy that says, "I was tested for STDs and I don't have anything." That is *not necessarily true!* He can't state that with certainty because he was not tested for *everything*. He most definitely was not tested for HPV.

You will not be able to claim that you are STD free either unless you get complete bacterial and viral STD testing. You only know results for the specific STDs you are tested for! And some of the viral STDs can be present in your body for a year or more before you would test positive. This means that it is not only important to know *if* a person has been tested, but how long it has been since that person last had sex! If it has not been *years,* the test results are unreliable.

Comment On This · Love This · Share with Friends

📝 **Note: To vaccinate or not to vaccinate? That is the question . . .** Recently, an HPV vaccine was made available for adolescent girls. Many of you are wondering, *Should I be vaccinated?* We obviously cannot make that decision for you, but we can pass along medical information to help you make a more informed choice. *Either way,* please understand that the vaccine is *not a cure* for HPV. To think that it makes sex safe is completely irrational. People are still putting themselves at risk for HPV, not to mention all other STDs, pregnancy and emotional pain.

HPV Vaccine Information. *What types of cancers does the vaccine protect against?* Most cancers of the vagina and vulva, and genital warts.

Does it protect against all strains of HPV? No, it will protect against four strains of the HPV—HPV-16, HPV-18, which account for approximately 70 percent of cervical cancer, as well as HPV-6 and HPV-11, which lead to about 90 percent of genital warts.[24] However, there are more than 100 HPV types,[25] more than 40 of which infect the genital area.[26] This means that cervical cancer, genital warts and HPV will still exist, so getting an annual pap smear will continue to be very important.

Who can take the vaccine? The FDA has approved the vaccine for women ages 9 through 26 years old. Recently the FDA approved the vaccine for males to prevent HPV-6 and HPV-11.[27]

How is it given? It is given in three doses over a period of six months.

Will it provide lifelong immunity? Since this is a fairly new vaccine it is not yet known. *If I am already infected with HPV will it work for me?* There is *no* evidence that this vaccine will work for people already infected. The vaccine works to prevent infection, not to treat precancerous conditions.[28]

Because the vaccine is fairly new, potential side effects are unknown. According to the FDA there have been some adverse events reported in vaccinated women.[29] Revised labeling indicates risks for fainting and suggests keeping patients for 15 minutes, because some individuals that have fainted have experienced seizure-like movements. So physical injury from falls is a concern. Additionally, some patients developed blood clots after vaccination, and 32 deaths were recorded, although their relationship to the vaccine is unknown.

You and your parent should discuss with your physician any questions or concerns that you have about this vaccine.

Myra: I didn't realize that the duration the vaccine was effective was unknown. Thank you for the information!

Comment On This · Love This · Share with Friends

Tonisha: I lost my virginity at 19. Since I waited longer than most of my friends, and they all seemed "fine," I didn't think it was a big deal to have sex. During my freshman year of college, I met the man I thought I would marry. We talked about where we would marry and who would be there and the type of ring I wanted. With all this conversation, I figured he was for sure "the one" and having sex was somehow more justified.

Two years later we still weren't married and I still didn't have a ring. What I did have was my OB/GYN office calling me to say my pap smear was abnormal and I needed to come in for more testing. And sure enough, I have HPV. To date I've had my cervix frozen twice. The boy is no longer in the picture and life feels dismal. Ironically, it isn't only because I have to tell my future spouse, but because every day I remember that special part of myself that I sacrificed.

My hope is that no one reading this will decide to get the vaccine because they think it will make sex outside of marriage safe. A vaccine does not give people a "green light" to premarital sex. Even if I hadn't gotten HPV, I'd still have to deal with all of the other consequences, including those to my heart and my soul, because I didn't honor God's boundary for sex.

Comment On This · Love This · Share with Friends

Pam: Tonisha, thank you for reminding everyone that sex is about more than just these diseases. It *deeply* involves the heart.

Comment On This · Love This · Share with Friends

💬 Denise's Story

I made many bad choices in my past, one of which left me with HPV that went undetected for years. By the time it was diagnosed I had cervical cancer. Because of that and other female problems, I had to undergo eight operations, the last being a complete hysterectomy at 28 years of age. The only pregnancy we ever had was lost at 12 weeks, on 9/11/99.

I suffered from low self-esteem and depression for many years as a teen and confused sex for love, turning to alcohol for comfort during those times to try to numb the pain. I cannot even tell you how many guys I was with.

After seeing your talk, the spirit of God moved me to begin sharing my story and encourage students to wait. I desperately wish someone had been there to speak truth to me years ago instead of just pushing birth control and condoms.

On a happy note, God blessed us with a beautiful child through adoption, on July 13, 2000, when our son was born. God is great!

Snapshot: Herpes simplex virus type 2

Nickname: Genital herpes

Category: Virus

Number infected: 45 million Americans[30]

How it is spread: Genital contact with an infected partner

What's the big deal: Transmission may occur even when a person doesn't have an active outbreak or even before they know they are infected. This disease is highly contagious and treatments only help suppress pain for blisters and boils. Transmission to newborns through vaginal deliveries have proven fatal, so infected mothers with active infections typically have to deliver their babies by cesarean section.

Paige: I was messing around with my boyfriend and we did oral on each other. Now I've noticed really painful red spots down there. Could I have gotten herpes?

Comment On This · Love This · Share with Friends

Pam: ORAL SEX IS SEX. The popular myth that oral sex is safe stems from the fact that your biggest fear is pregnancy. *If we do "everything but" vaginal intercourse, we won't get pregnant and we will be "safe."* But herpes and all the other STDs previously discussed are transmitted via oral sex. This means that anyone who has had oral sex is at risk for infection, and you will need to let every future partner know about every person you've had oral sex with.

Comment On This · Love This · Share with Friends

@ **Link comment:** If you've been watching TV at all lately you've seen the commercial where the beautiful girl jumps off her bike and says, "I have genital herpes." Birds are singing, she's smiling and her life looks perfect, painless and carefree. NOT TRUE! Read this woman's story: http://std.about.com/u/ua/herpes/herpesuserstories.htm.[31]

I got herpes from one of two guys I was fooling around with. And until it happens to you, you think you are invincible. I never thought anything like this would happen. This is so horrible. I can't sit. It's hard to stand. I have a two-year-old that I can hardly play with because I can't bend or anything.

This is awful. I cry every day because I feel so helpless. *Why me?* I ask myself. No one deserves this. It has taught me a huge lesson in the fact that your life can change in a split second. I thought I could just fool around and nothing would ever happen. Well, it did.

Liz: Holy cow! I had no idea herpes was such a painful disease. Reading that story was a huge eye-opener!
Comment On This · Love This · Share with Friends

📰 **Newsflash:** 1 in 5 Americans over the age of 12 is infected with herpes.[32]

Pam: *Never* take your health for granted. This is about your life. This is about your relationships. This is about your future. If you have crossed the line, GET TESTED!
Comment On This · Love This · Shares with Friends

Ellen: I've had sex a few times and have never noticed anything "down there." How long does it take for a disease to show up?
Comment On This · Love This · Shares with Friends

Pam: I'm glad that you asked. You *cannot* judge whether or not you have a disease by just looking or by a lack of symptoms. In fact, 80 percent of the people infected with sexually transmitted diseases *have no symptoms*.[33] That is four out of five! People are not running around infecting each other because they mean to. They are infecting each other because they do not know they are infected.
Comment On This · Love This · Share with Friends

Natasha: Where could I go to get good testing for free? If my parents knew that I had sex they would kill me. I need to fly under the radar with this one.
Comment On This · Love This · Shares with Friends

Pam: You have no idea how many times I've heard the words "my parents are going to kill me," and yet in my all my years of counseling I have never lost a client to death by parents! Who are we kidding here? Your concern is not that your parents will kill you. Your concern is that you will lose your parents' trust, which your actions indicate you *don't deserve* right now anyway, and that you will have to pay consequences. Travel with me a few years down the road. Don't you think having your parents "upset" would be far better than suffering from severe pelvic inflammatory disease and finding yourself infertile because of a bacteria that you could have treated with antibiotics if only you had told the people that you were too scared to tell?

Anonymous testing places you at the mercy of *less than ideal* medical care. While the intent may be to help, the government simply cannot afford to test everyone for everything. So they would probably test you for Chlamydia and HIV and possibly give you a pap smear, but there is *so much more* that you need to know. What about the other diseases? What if your body is harboring a disease that isn't showing up yet and you don't have follow-up care planned? What if the test is positive? The "free" clinic normally does not provide "treatment" for major problems like cervical cancer; they just do the testing!

If you are under the care of a good OB/GYN or family practice physician you can use your insurance to get more thorough testing. He or she would also have your sexual history in your medical file so that if you experience a symptom or difficulty that could be STD-related they are aware and can appropriately follow up. Furthermore, if you test positive for a disease, it would be in your permanent chart to help ensure the best long-term healthcare.

Please don't compromise your future health. Tell your parents. Go to your doctor. Be honest about your sexual history. Get tested now. And be sure to follow through with any future testing your physician orders.

Comment On This · Love This · Share with Friends

Pam: "Take care of your body. It's the only place you have to live." —Jim Rohn

Comment On This · Love This · Shares with Friends

Chapter 6

When Chemistry Is More than a Subject:
The Heart's Broken Bonds

Pam: Sex is more than just a biological act to meet a biological need. It is more than a few body parts touching. Sex involves your *MIND* and your *HEART*. And, there is no condom, pill or vaccine in the world that can protect you from the intense emotional pain that can follow if you choose to have sex outside of marriage.

Comment On This · Love This · Shares with Friends

Marissa: I messed up by having oral sex with my boyfriend. It was the first genital contact either of us had with another person. Still, we went for STD testing and were both told that we are STD free. At the time, that brought me relief, but today I am just one big mess. My boyfriend and I broke up and suddenly I get why people say you should save all this stuff for marriage. I still have a lot of very strong feelings for him and, quite honestly, I almost feel like I own a little part of him because he has that part of me now. It frustrates me that I feel attached to a boy that I am not even with anymore.

Comment On This · Love This · Share with Friends

Deanna: I understand. I dated this wonderful guy for about a year. We didn't even have sex. But, he was the first guy that I kissed. Although it felt magical to me it was apparently not so magical to him. He said that "we weren't right together" and yesterday I saw him kiss his new girlfriend in the hallway at school! I know there are other guys out there for me, but I feel so connected to him that I find it hard to just move on.

Comment On This · Love This · Share with Friends

Christine: Wow. I'm glad that I read this today. Earlier today my boyfriend broke up with me. He said that I was too conservative and that he didn't want me to compromise my standards and re- gret it but he really did want to have "fun" and that would be a prob- lem when we were together. In my head, I know that we shouldn't be together, but the breakup stung so bad. As the end of the school day neared, I started thinking that maybe what he wants isn't really a big deal and that I should just go along with it. He doesn't want to have sex. He wants to have "fun." Your comments were just the reality check I needed. I might think I'm hurting now, but I would be hurting a whole lot more if I let something happen!

Comment On This · Love This · Share with Friends

 Emily: You came to my school in the beginning of the year, and I was so inspired by your speech. I promised to not have sex until marriage and am still committed to keeping that promise. I've had the same boyfriend for over a year now, and I'm only in ninth grade. And I know a lot of people probably say this, but I really do love him with all my heart. He is completely aware of my promise and we've talked about it and he is totally okay with it. But as I'm getting deeper into high school I'm realizing how hard it will be to only kiss and nothing else.

Everyone is surprised when they hear we've only been to first base after being together so long. My boyfriend gets a lot of flack from his friends about it and I'm starting to think it's not as much of a realistic goal as I thought. It seems like it comes up more and more in my conversations. I don't want to be pressured by anyone, but it's kind of overwhelming at times. And, the thing is, I don't think we are breaking up anytime soon . . . and what if I want to do more? I'm just really confused as to what to do. Is going to second base bad? PLEASE HELP.

BTW, my parents aren't too happy about me having a boyfriend for so long when I'm so young. They don't get how close we are and that we really do love each other. Sometimes it makes things hard. What should I do?

Any help you could give me would be great. Thanks so much.

Comment On This · Love This · Shares with Friends

 Pam: You have just described perfectly the reason that dating at your age is so difficult. As a mom, I did not allow my children to date at all until they were 16, and *NEVER* alone until they graduated from high school.

I am not questioning your feelings. I am sure they are very real. However, neither of you is in any position to get married in the next four years (probably longer), so you have put yourself in a position that requires you to fight off temptation for a very long time. It will take a tremendous amount of character. Unfortunately, moving the boundary *NOW* will just make it more and more difficult to keep the *NEW* boundary. Second base leads to *THIRD* base, which leads to going "all the way" with each compromise being justified until you have given *ALL* of yourself and can no longer look at the relationship with a critical eye.

Every physical act (hugging, holding hands, kissing) has the ability to release a neurochemical in your brain called "oxytocin." His primary neurochemical is called "vasopressin," which behaves differently than the "bonding" chemical in women. I know this sounds like science, but I think it is important you understand this. Oxytocin, released in your brain, was designed by God to help you "bond." It's also released at the onset of labor and when you are nursing a baby to help a mother bond emotionally with her child.

The more you engage in this intimate activity with this boy the more your "brain" will be bonded to him. This is all good if you are married. It helps a married couple keep the very difficult promise of "till death do us part." Here is the problem—the chances that you will be with this boyfriend "until death do you part" are slim. And the question of whether you SHOULD even be with him at your age is still open for debate. The breaking up of a relationship in which your brain has "bonded" in this way can be extremely painful and leave damage to your ability to bond with your future husband.

You absolutely *MUST* take this seriously. The consequences of falling to this temptation and getting more involved physically are not just consequences of disease or pregnancy. This will affect your ability to have a healthy and happy marriage.

Until you prove that you have the maturity to *KEEP* your standards—and *KEEP THEM STRICTLY* (NO making out, and certainly NO touching of the genitals, clothed or not)—you are *NOT* ready to date. As painful as it might seem, you would be MUCH better off not dating at all than taking this HUGE risk of damaging your body, brain, soul and spirit!

Be honest with yourself and be honest with him. If he is pressuring you *AT ALL,* you must end it!

Comment On This · Love This · Share with Friends

📰 **Newsflash:** The average high school couple will last 21 days after having sex.[1]

📝 **Note: What's the Story with These Neurochemicals?** If you're like many teenagers these days, you've probably rushed out to the movie theater to see the box office hit *Alice in Wonderland.* In the film, Alice encounters a bottle marked "Drink Me." Curious and tempted, Alice does just that and, outside of her control, she immediately shrinks. Once that happens, life becomes complicated. The neurochemicals in your brain are like that potion. Once you induce their effect you are instantaneously changed.

Perhaps you or your friends have claimed, "It was my hormones. They were out of control." But *YOU* are in control of your body. Hormones and neurochemicals don't just take over. To a certain degree, you *ALLOW* them to through choices you make.

If we take the time to understand how these neurochemicals are stimulated and their effects, you can set the boundary far enough back that you do not get overcome or damaged by their powerful response.

Oxytocin. Present in both males and females but more profoundly impacts female bonding. Romantic touch (as simple as a hug) for as few as 20 seconds can trigger oxytocin release.[2] "It is an involuntary process that cannot distinguish between a one-night stand and a lifelong soul mate. Oxytocin can cause a woman to bond to a man even during what was expected to be a short-term sexual relationship."[3] Once the oxytocin release occurs, females bond with the male "creating a greater desire to be near him and most significantly, place greater trust in him."[4] If you have sex with multiple people you will "diminish the power of oxytocin to maintain a permanent bond with an individual."[5]

Girls, understand the POINT! Once you allow yourself to get into a situation where oxytocin is released outside of marriage you become bonded in an unhealthy way to an unhealthy partner. The desire it generates to be physically close rather than innocently "hang out together" *CHANGES* the focus of your relationship and reduces your ability to say no. The bond is not one that you choose. It *WILL HAPPEN* because of the neurochemical release. Not only does this inhibit your ability to bond most powerfully with your spouse alone, but it will set you up for deeper felt pain in a breakup.

Vasopressin. Floods male during intercourse causing him to partially bond. Nicknamed the "monogamy hormone." Studies indicate this chemical release will increase the male's attentiveness towards his mate.[6]

At this point, vasopressin is not as widely studied as oxytocin, but *UNDERSTAND*, boys, the effect that you have on women and that they have on you. If you allow yourself to emotionally bond through a sexual relationship with a girl that you are not married to, you could very possibly find yourself overattached to a girl that you ARE NOT MEANT TO BE WITH. These chemicals will cloud your thinking! Beyond that, you will be partially responsible for a *VERY EMOTIONALLY BONDED* female. (Does the word "clingy" come to mind?) YOU need to be warriors for the purity of the girls around you. We're challenging you to be counterculture. BE ADVOCATES for healthy boundaries and treat girls with respect so that you can experience the goodness of God's design!

 Dina: This was really interesting. A few months ago I lost my virginity to my boyfriend. Shortly thereafter we broke up and I'm still pretty attached. Many nights I can't sleep or I find myself crying in my room because I can't let my feelings for him go. I always wondered if boys get attached, because it killed me inside to think that he wouldn't care. I guess now I get it.

Comment On This · Love This · Share with Friends

Pam: Boys are not emotionally void. They have feelings and are influenced by their relationships. Unfortunately, once these chemicals are kicked into gear it becomes very easy to confuse "deep caring" with "love." And, for girls, the powerful, biologically created bond makes walking away difficult. That is why having an *AWARENESS* of these chemicals and the way they work in your body is critical. I pray that you will first STOP having sex until you are married to break the power of these bonds and, secondly, that you will use this knowledge to set healthy boundaries in the future. Eliminating the physical contact will help *YOU BE IN CONTROL* rather than having your hormones *TAKE CONTROL OF YOU.*

Comment On This · Love This · Share with Friends

❣ Landon's Story

My girlfriend and I dated for nearly a year before deciding to have sex. In our minds, it would bring us closer together and make our relationship perfect. Oh how wrong we were. A few minutes of pleasure was quickly followed by fear, arguments and complications.

Now that we've had sex my girlfriend expects that we will get married. All of this has me stressed and, ironically, what was intended to bring us closer together has caused me to distance myself from her. Still, I find even myself confused because I feel like I am obligated to marry her because I had sex with her. Sin is sin, but somehow in my head the idea of marrying her would make me feel more right with God. Man, this has my thinking twisted.

I feel so guilty. We were much better off before we had sex. Now no answer seems like a right answer. And, the killer is we could have prevented all of this if we just would have stayed away from the physical stuff.

📰 Newsflash: Two out of three sexually experienced teens wish that they would have waited longer before having sex.[7]

Pam: For many years people have believed that they could "sow their wild oats" before marriage and then once they said, "I do" they would be able to control what they never controlled before. The result has been pain, increased divorce rates, and marital infidelity. The choices you make *TODAY* will impact your *TOMORROW!*

Comment On This · Love This · Shares with Friends

Phil: Your comment hit home for me. I've been married three times. Prior to my marriages, I had several one-night stands. Like everyone else, I didn't think it mattered. It was just a "good time." I cheated on both my first wife and my second wife. I'm not really like that though. I'm not sure why I did it. Although I'm happy with my current wife, my kids' world has been shaken. They go from home to home and, since they know what I did, they don't really trust me.

Comment On This · Love This · Share with Friends

 Pam: I'm so sorry for the devastation that your family has experienced. Regrettably, your family is not alone. From secrets locked within people's hearts to the very public Tiger Woods story, families everywhere are picking up pieces of shattered lives caused by irresponsible sexual choices.

Please get counseling. Your "I'm not like that" comment indicates *SERIOUS* denial. Do you think you were having an out-of-body experience? Who was involved in these indiscretions? Your "other" self? NO! It was *YOU.* Unless you invest time in strengthening your character, choices and behaviors, you will be setting yourself up for another affair and divorce number three, wounding yet one more woman and amplifying your children's distrust in you. The stakes are high, Phil. I hope you'll do what is right.

Comment On This · Love This · Share with Friends

📰 **Newflash:** Individuals who engage in premarital sexual activity are 50 percent more likely to divorce later in life than those who do not.[8]

 Mary: I had sex with two guys before I was married. To be quite honest, I was pretty impressed with myself. Most of my friends had more partners than I did. When I got married, I was expecting the sex to be awesome. But, I was wrong. As much as I hate to admit it, it doesn't seem that much different than my previous relationships. Why? I mean, he's "the one."

Comment On This · Love This · Shares with Friends

 Pam: When God designed sex, He did so with elaborate detail. Since it was meant for marriage He thought, *I can make this about more than physical parts feeling good. I will create a chemical response that will tie them together even when they are apart.* For a married couple that has abstained from sex, this is brilliant. Their "one flesh" experience is just that. Oxytocin enhances the love and binds the trust. And, vasopressin generates an almost jealous protection that says, "You are mine."

If on the other hand, God's handiwork is abused, this involuntary physiological response will bond you to whomever you are with.

Given time and too many partners this bond will lose its power. However, this doesn't mean that you can't have meaningful sex with your husband. Seeing a good Christian marriage counselor would help you and your husband work through some of the past relationships and breakups that gave birth to these feelings.

Comment On This · Love This · Share with Friends

@ **Link:** I was flipping through radio stations and was struck by Reba McEntire's song "She Thinks His Name Was John." (You can find a link to the song on the *Nobody Told Me* Facebook fan page.) Talk about a bleeding heart! She can't let go of a man's image from a one-night stand years after the choice.

 Naomi: My name is Naomi Colback, and I am writing from Australia. The problem expressed in this song is a problem worldwide. When sex happens outside of marriage there is great pain of the soul involved. If you have sex with someone or are sexually impure, and your soul and their soul join, you are "glued together." Then, when you leave that person, you take a part of their soul and they take a part of yours. This part you can never get back and you can never give to the person God created for you. *Sex* is *serious!*

People need to start talking about this in a godly way. If the media and everywhere we look are open to sex and sexual immorality in an ungodly way, then why won't God's people step up and be preachers of the Word and His truth?

Sex is *holy*. Sex is *sacred*. Sex is an act of *worship* to *God*. Sex is two souls coming together like glue. Sex is *not* just physical. Sex is *pure*. Sex is *intimate*. Sex brings two people together *spiritually*. Sex can be *powerful*. God intended sex to be *only* between husband and wife.

Comment On This · Love This · Share with Friends

 Pam: You are absolutely correct! Early in my speaking career, when I was speaking in classrooms, I would take duct tape or packing tape with me to illustrate this point that you have so well articulated. Telling the students that sex has the ability to "bond" two people together just like this tape, I would take a big piece of tape and wrap it around my arm. It would stick pretty well the first time I did it. Then, I would rip it off! Pieces of my skin would come off on the back of the tape. Next, I'd stick it to one of the student's arms. It would stick a little. Not as good as the first time, but it would stick a bit. When I ripped it off of their arm, I'd have "junk" from my arm *and* their am on the back of the tape. I continued this process until the tape would stick to *nothing* at all. It had collected so much skin and hair and dead cells until it completely lost its "stickiness." God gives us an incredible gift, our sexuality, to be shared with our spouse. If that gift is mistreated, we hold on to the junk of past relationships forever. It *is* powerful!

Comment On This · Love This · Share with Friends

 Hadley: My boyfriend and I dated for a month before we decided to have sex. After that everything changed. Every time we would get together it seems like we did it either out of temptation or simple expectation. Our communication has drastically decreased to the point where we barely even talk. We just get physical. I don't really want to say it to him, but I feel like we have nothing left. I don't know anything about him and he doesn't know anything about me. We are just body buds. I don't know what to do.

Comment On This · Love This · Shares with Friends

 Pam: Sex was never meant to "create intimacy." It was meant to be an *expression* of intimacy that already existed. When we introduce sex into a relationship that is just beginning, without any permanent commitment (marriage) and then hope that the sex will itself "create" intimacy, we have put the proverbial cart before the horse. Intimacy is work. It requires two people selflessly opening up to one another and learning to trust. We go from sharing "facts" about ourselves to sharing our feelings to sharing our hopes and dreams. As we learn to communicate at deep levels, we share not only common interests but also a common "mission." If sex is introduced into a relationship that has not had the time to "learn" true intimacy, it becomes a bad substitute for the beautiful expression of an intimacy that already exists in a relationship built on trust and a permanent commitment to the other.

Comment On This · Love This · Share with Friends

 Pam: You can survive without sex, but you might struggle to survive if you have sex outside of marriage.

Comment On This · Love This · Shares with Friends

 Jessica: You got that right. I'm a straight-*A*, alcohol-free "good girl" that people believe has it all together. But I made a decision two weeks ago that I totally regret. I had sex for the first time. After my boyfriend left, I cried and cried. When I was on the phone with him, the tears came like a waterfall. That freaked my boyfriend out and so he broke up with me.

A couple of nights later my ex showed up at my bedroom window. I still cared for him and I wanted to believe that he still cared for me. He came in, and I gave in. It was so weird because it was like I knew that I shouldn't, but that rational side of me battled with the emotional side that was screaming, "This is love." Then we broke up again.

This has put me over the edge. I want to end my life so I don't have to bear this load. I'm scared. I'm scared of what people might think when word gets around. I'm scared about what my mom will say. I'm deathly afraid of STDs. And I wish I had never fallen for him in the first place.

Comment On This · Love This · Share with Friends

Lynn: You are not alone. I feel like my past has made me feel empty inside.

Comment On This · Love This · Share with Friends

Pam: Jessica, if you are seriously contemplating ending your life, PLEASE tell an adult in your life and be honest about your feelings. Here is a hotline number to call for help: 1-800-273-TALK as well. I know that life feels bleak for both of you right now, but there *is* hope in Christ! He can walk you through this and lead you to a place of health and wholeness again *if* you are willing to take the first step.

Comment On This · Love This · Share with Friends

📰 **Newsflash:** Sexually active boys were nearly nine times more likely, and teen girls three times more likely, to attempt suicide than their peers who abstain.[9]

Angela: I am struggling right now too, but in a different way. I've had sex with several guys. Sometimes they were people that I'd been dating and the others, honestly, were just a result of being an "easy" catch because I'd had a few too many drinks. Anyway, having had sex has resulted in my craving sex. I am seriously obsessed. When I am not having it I am thinking about it or masturbating or anything that will make me feel right. I desperately need to get control of this. I feel depressed when I'm not sexually gratified—like I'm worth nothing or something.

Comment On This · Love This · Shares with Friends

Pam: Angela, you *are* worth something. You are worth SO MUCH MORE than this meaningless sex.

First things first, you *need* to be tested for STDs. Please call your physician's office and get that scheduled. Then, call a Christian counselor. In the midst of these unhealthy hookups you have formed an addiction to sex. Until you break that addiction—through intense counseling, zero pornography, no dating, and abstinence—you *will not* feel better *nor* will you really feel gratified. These relationships are shallow. They may bring physical gratification for the moment, but because they are empty of intimacy they leave you unsatisfied.

The pornography adds to your struggle. You might think that it is innocent voyeurism, but it sexually stimulates you, and having that stimulation will only *add* to your difficulty in respecting healthy boundaries when you do date again. It needs to go. Disconnect from the Internet and toss out the movies, images and books that are causing you to fall. This is your *life* we are talking about!

The God who made the heavens and the earth made *you*. He loves you and longs for you to experience love from His perspective. Please turn your eyes to Him and get good help. If you do not know the name of someone, please call 1-800-395-HELP and your local pregnancy care center will meet with you free of charge and help connect you with the best counselor in your community.

Comment On This · Love This · Share with Friends

💬 Danielle's Story

I waited to date until my junior year of high school. Right away, my boyfriend and I established a boundary, agreeing that we didn't want to have sex until we were married. As our relationship continued, I felt pressured to do other things with him. After all, I didn't want him to think that I was boring.

To be honest, I wasn't sure what was really considered sex and what wasn't. My boyfriend didn't really know either, and both of us fell for the societal lie that if it is anything but intercourse it is okay. Needless to say, we made choices that I now regret.

Once in a while I break down in tears. At the age of 14, I promised God that I would wait until I was married, and I even hoped that my first boyfriend would be my husband. Looking back, I set myself up for failure. He didn't even know the Lord. Why would I expect that he would have the same standards? I guess I believed we were in love and love would be enough.

A year ago we broke up. I spiraled down into a huge depression. My heart was broken, and I really didn't care to do anything. I didn't understand why. We didn't have sex. But with the help of a counselor, I discovered that I was so hurt and upset because I'd never accepted that I had, in fact, lost my virginity, and I finally understood that my "innocent" actions could cause a lot of pain. I felt worthless, and many days I still do. But I love God, and He is getting me through day by day.

Newsflash: Depression runs so high in sexually active teens that doctors are advised to have all their at-risk population screened.[10]

Dayne: After dating my girlfriend for two years, I gave her my virginity. It wasn't long after that that we realized our relationship wasn't as healthy as we thought. So, we broke up. It might not sound "manly" to some of my friends, but I honestly struggle daily because I have given away the one thing that was truly mine. I've started going back to church, but it hasn't "fixed" it like I thought it would. I've made a vow to myself and God that I will never make this mistake again, but I don't know how to deal with these feelings that I'm having right now. Why do I feel dirty and so, so empty?

Comment On This · Love This · Shares with Friends

Pam: I want to thank you for being "manly" and sharing the *truth*. From an emotional standpoint, it is going to take time to heal from this relationship. You did give her a piece of yourself and that "loss" isn't going to go away overnight or even with a couple trips to church. But a *broken* heart over your choices and the pain that you are experiencing are a *good* thing because you have acknowledged that what happened was wrong, and the pain will remind you to make wiser choices in the future.

Because you go to church, you know that *none* of us is perfect. We have all sinned and all experienced pain. BUT, God loved us so much that He *knew* we would need redemption, and He selflessly took on the pain through Jesus' death on the cross to free us from our sin and shame. You have told God that you are sorry and you have repented over your sin, and now He has *given you a clean slate!* His Word tells us that He has thrown our sin as far as the east is from the west (see Psalm 103:12). Since the King has forgiven you, it is now time that you forgive yourself. Healing *will come* in time!

Comment On This · Love This · Share with Friends

Pam: If, after spending some time thinking about God's plan for sexuality and marriage, you are now realizing that you have made mistakes, *there is hope for you!* Please ask for forgiveness from your heavenly Father who is waiting with open arms for you to return to Him.

Comment On This · Love This · Shares with Friends

SECTION THREE:

Where Do We Go from Here?

Chapter 7

Repentance and Renewal: Rewriting Your Story

 Pam: If you have had sex, today you have a *very important* choice to make. You can ignore all that you've learned here and continue to make choices that will put your future at risk. Or, you can run into the arms of Jesus who loves you and say, "I'm sorry. From this day forward I will honor You, myself and my future spouse by recycled virginity."

Comment On This · Love This · Shares with Friends

 Taryn: Thank you for this! A year ago, I was at a party and made a decision to get in the backseat of a car with a boy that I had just met. One thing led to another and we started having sex. I quickly realized what I was doing and left. To this day, I regret drinking. I regret giving my virginity to a stranger. I have to live with this decision even though I desperately wish that I could rewind time and take it back. I'm not a bad person, but I did make some bad choices. I really wasn't sure if it was okay to move on or even possible to restart my life, but you have reminded me and everyone else that we can! I feel like a giant weight has been lifted off of my shoulders.

Comment On This · Love This · Share with Friends

 Rachel: I'm just going to admit it. I fell on the wrong side of the track. My boyfriend and I had sex many times. We broke up and I hurt, but I thought it would be no big deal. I'd get over it. In my head it wasn't the sex that hurt me, it was the breakup. Shortly thereafter I got into another relationship, had sex and, like the first boyfriend, broke up. Again, I was in pain. I knew that God didn't want this for my life but I didn't really care. I thought it made me desirable, and I wanted that.

It wasn't until I was in my sixth relationship that I realized my breakups were hurting me far more than what my friends who were virgins were experiencing in not having relationships. And when I would go on double dates with my abstinent friends, I watched them interact with their dates. I noticed how much more they had to talk about. More surprisingly, it seemed that the way their dates looked at them actually made me feel like they were more desirable to their dates than I was to the boys I was giving sex to. I couldn't believe it. When I talked to my friend about it, she rolled her eyes and said, "Well, duh! There is mystery in the wait that makes us appreciate each other more."

That hit me smack in the face. I'd never thought about that mystery being intriguing until she said it. But, of course it makes sense. They are holding out because they care so much for each other that they are sharing their hopes, dreams and values; and in the process of finding people that they could potentially marry there is excitement, beauty and love.

I'm done with my old ways. It's been two years. I get it, and I want God's best!

Comment On This · Love This · Share with Friends

Pam: Thanks so much, girls, for sharing your stories and encouraging words! You have made a GREAT CHOICE! Remember, the *value* of sexuality is shown in how you value *yourself!* You are all children to the King of kings! Expect the respect you so rightly deserve!

Comment On This · Love This · Share with Friends

Jada: After reading your status update and the shared stories, I must admit that I am still struggling. You say to repent, but it doesn't feel that simple. I lost my virginity and I've asked for forgiveness of that sin. In fact, I find myself pleading with God every night for this, but I still feel guilty. Despite going to church my whole life, I can't just run into His arms and say, "I'm sorry," because I have doubts about His love for me after committing this particular sin. Will I always feel guilty?

Comment On This · Love This · Shares with Friends

Pam: All of us have doubted whether or not God can forgive us. Understanding the vast love of the Father—a love that is so contrary to the way the world loves—is challenging. After all, we are human. We struggle.

Scripture says that "If we confess our sins, he is faithful and just and will forgive us our sins and purify us from all unrighteousness" (1 John 1:9). In the midst of this guilt, you are confusing "*being* forgiven" with "*feeling* forgiven." It is part of spiritual maturity that we begin to *trust the truth* without necessarily trusting how we *feel*. If you have confessed your sin; taken responsibility for your actions, without blaming others or your circumstances for your choices; and asked for forgiveness, YOU ARE FORGIVEN. You have been washed clean.

This does *not* mean that there will be no *consequences*. Even with confession and abundant forgiveness you may still carry physical and emotional scars. But Christ has overcome the world (see John 16:33) and one day we will be *completely freed* of all the consequences of our past. That place is called *heaven*.

From your post, I can tell that you are really struggling to get past this one sin. Perhaps you would find it helpful to have a tangible expression of your forgiveness and healing. For some it is as simple as putting the date of your repentance and decision for re-cycled virginity inside your Bible. Or it could be something as big as planting a tree in your yard, painting or drawing a picture to hang in your room, or writing a poem or song to place on your mirror. Whatever reminder is a fit for you, seal the date that you have put your past in the *past*.

Move forward in freedom, Jada, because Christ has set you free!

· Comment On This · Love This · Share with Friends

📰 **Newsflash:** "God allows U-turns! And you have the chance to make one right now. Make a commitment beginning now that you will not have sex again until your wedding night."[1]

 Pam: Breaking the bonds from your sexual past is like changing your underwear. It must be done or life's going to stink!
Comment On This · Love This · Share with Friends

 Gretta: I've dated my boyfriend for three years. When we started dating, we both clearly stated that we had no interest in being sexually active before marriage. As time passed, we got too comfortable with one another and we started crossing boundaries. Now we don't know how to get out of this evil cycle where we will get caught up in the moment, start to have sex and then quickly back away. Afterwards, we both feel guilty and have the same discussion over and over again about how we have to stop. We are Christians and don't want to mess up anymore. Is it too late?
Comment On This · Love This · Shares with Friends

 Pam: It is *never* too late. You *can* stop if you take the proper steps. First of all, you both need to *choose* to honor the "no genital contact" boundary. Since being alone has placed you in tempting situations, you *need* to keep your dates in public places until the sexual bonds that are driving you to have sex are broken. You should *not* be alone together. Furthermore, you should plan your dates down to the last minute. Having "free time" is dangerous!

You can take some of the pressure off by including other couples on your dates. Because you will be in the presence of others, it will keep your conversations clean and healthy so that you do not lead one another into risky territory.

On Sundays, I would encourage you to attend church together. Hearing God's Word and having time to reflect about it will lift your thinking above your wants and desires to what God wants and desires for you. This will not only enrich your conversations and prayer life together, but it will also open your eyes to right from wrong.

Finally, I would encourage you to visit a pregnancy care center. Even if you do not fear pregnancy, you both need to sit down and discuss your relationship. They can walk you through relationship/abstinence counseling, and in doing so you will be made aware of your relationship's strengths and weaknesses. Through this discovery process, you will learn if you are right for one another or if you are holding on to the relationship for the wrong reasons.

Dealing with temptation is difficult, but we don't need to make it *more* difficult by constantly putting ourselves in the middle of temptation. First Corinthians 10:13 says, "No temptation has seized you except what is common to man. And God is faithful; he will not let you be tempted beyond what you can bear. But when you are tempted, he will also provide a way out so that you can stand up under it." Did you get that? God *promises* us a way of escape from temptation. It seems that the problem is we don't *use* it! It's like standing on a set of railroad tracks with a train barreling down on you while you pray fervently for God to stop the train! GET OFF THE TRACKS! These practical steps will help you find your way of escape.

Comment On This · Love This · Share with Friends

🐦 **Note: Breaking the Bonds.** First Corinthians 6:16 of *THE MESSAGE* reads, "There's more to sex than mere skin on skin. Sex is as much spiritual mystery as physical fact. As written in Scripture, 'The two become one.' Since we want to become spiritually one with the Master, we must not pursue the kind of sex that avoids commitment and intimacy, leaving us more lonely than ever—the kind of sex that can never 'become one.'"

When you have sex with someone, you have bonded with that person, even if you didn't intend to do so. It's not just a physical act that you can walk away from unchanged. Even with time, these bonds aren't easily broken. In order to free yourself from the past entangling you, you must consciously choose to break past bonds.

Take some time to think through all of the inappropriate sexual bonds that you may have made in your life. If it helps, you might want to write down names or circumstances on a piece of paper. As these people or incidents come into your mind, ask God to forgive you, if necessary, for the part that you played in creating the bond. If it was abuse or rape, please ask God for the grace to forgive the person who harmed you. And then, ask God to free you from any bond or spiritual harm that may have come to you as a result of those circumstances.

Barbara Wilson offers a great prayer tool to help you break past sexual bonds:

Lord, I ask forgiveness for sinning against You and against my own body. In the name of Jesus, I sever and renounce the bonds I have created with _____. I release my heart tie with this person physically, emotionally, and spiritually. I choose by faith to forgive _____ for his (or her) violation against me. Please forgive my violation against _____. Please remove my baggage I've been carrying around with me. Restore to me a virgin heart—as though I'd never been with this person, and heal me completely of the damage this sin has caused me now or could cause in the future. Thank You for Your forgiveness. I accept it fully. Amen. [2]

For any of you whose faith allows for and encourages sacramental confession, it would be powerful to include the thoughts Wilson's prayer surfaced in your heart in the sacrament of reconciliation.

Now rip up your list! Burn it! Bury it! *Destroy* it!

Once you have experienced this confession and healing, please memorize these verses so that you can easily bring them to mind every time the enemy tries to drudge up the pain of your past or tell you that you are not forgiven.

You will again have compassion on us; you will tread our sins underfoot and hurl all our iniquities into the depths of the sea (Micah 7:19).

In him we have redemption through his blood, the forgiveness of sins, in accordance with the riches of God's grace (Ephesians 1:7).

 Gina: I loved these practical steps. You see, I always intended to remain pure and knew that God would help me defy any worldly pressure. I let others know that being a virgin was okay because I was one and I was happy. But I was living a lie. I had no idea that oral sex was truly *sex,* and I'd fallen to that sexual sin. After learning that it was, I felt sick. Although I immediately quit the behavior, I have been tormented over this for more than two years. I pushed it back and hid it in the depths of my soul. The only problem was, whenever I would even start to date a guy, guilt would engulf me. If I married him, how would I tell him? I couldn't let it go. This finally helped me to do so!

Comment On This · Love This · Share with Friends

💗 Lindsey's Story

When I was 16, I met and started dating my boyfriend. To my surprise, I quickly fell for him. He was committed but didn't feel like we needed to be together 24/7. I loved that about him. I could focus on basketball or go to the mall with my girlfriends and he never pressured me to give him more of my time. He focused on football and his studies and, together, we were your all-American couple, making good grades and close to our families.

I don't date guys unless they are someone that I could see myself marrying. At 18, we are still together.

After dating just one year, we started having sex. Neither of us had ever had sex before, and it was very special . . . or so we thought. What we didn't realize was how this would influence our relationship. Suddenly, it was like he worried about me more. He always wanted to know where I was going to be and with whom. Oppositely, I struggled most when I was with him. Did he just want to talk and play cards like before or was he thinking that we should be having sex? I never felt comfortable.

This bothered me and I didn't want to ruin any potential future we had together. So I talked with my boyfriend. We were to the point where we were having sex nearly every time we were together, so I had no idea how he would respond. Would he dump me? Would he be mad? Would he be relieved? Every possibility ran through my head. To my surprise, it was the latter. It was amazing. He agreed, and we stopped having sex that day.

Today marks eight months of sexual abstinence, and it feels like we have grown even closer because instead of having sex we talk. The tension that cropped up in our relationship has disappeared. And both of us feel that our relationship is healthier.

Honestly, it was hard to stop for me. But I am living proof that it can be done. It is never too late!

 Dara: My sophomore year of high school I met this wonderful guy and I lost my virginity to him, knowing that it was wrong and that God would be disappointed. The attention felt good, so I turned my back on God. I chose him over my Father. The problem was, I didn't really have a relationship with God. I just believed in this far-off God who gave me a list of rules about what to do and not to do.

Now I've been going to youth group and I've finally found the relationship with Christ that I never had. So, I told my boyfriend that I wanted to stop having sex, and he said, "After all this time you want to stop?" He looks at sex as a normal thing that is okay to do with someone if you are dating; but I now see it as a wonderful thing I should've waited for. What do I do? Do I really break up with a guy that's been good to me for two-and-a-half years, because I want to stop? Truthfully, I don't know if I can do that even though I know that I should.

Comment On This · Love This · Shares with Friends

Pam: First of all, guarding your *heart* can be as difficult as guarding your *body*. Your hesitation to break up indicates that you are allowing *feelings* to determine *truth* rather than making truth direct your feelings!

Let's deal with what seems to be *true*:

First, he is being disrespectful of you and your feelings. I know that "attention" might feel good, but it seems you are seeking "attention" from a very wrong source. *Not all attention is positive.*

Second, no relationship is healthy when it causes you pain. It would seem like this is more of an "obsession" than a relationship. Sorry to break it to you, but his words translate this way: "I am with you because we are having sex with each other." If you don't believe me, set a "no genital contact" boundary and see if he sticks around.

Trying to grow in your faith while navigating the waters of this relationship is not a good plan. Perhaps a better use of this time would be spent worrying about *who you are*. If you want a godly man, then you need to become a godly woman. To do this, you need to focus your heart on Christ alone. Bask in His attention. My Bible says the Lord cherishes you this way: "I have loved you with an everlasting love; I have drawn you with loving-kindness" (Jeremiah 31:3). You want love? God has the real deal. You want a tender embrace? His arms are safe. As you study the Word and nurture your newly formed relationship with Christ, transformation will occur in *your character* and you will *attract* godly men.

Once you are back in the world, your "choices" will be limited, but believe me when I say patience will bring a *great* reward! The right one is out there and will be worthy of the wait!

Comment On This · Love This · Share with Friends

@ Link: For any of you questioning the heart of God as you make decisions about recycled virginity, read this portion of "Father's Love Letter!"[3] (http://www.fatherslove letter.com/text.html). A link is also available on the *Nobody Told Me* Facebook fan page.

Every good gift that you receive comes from my hand (James 1:17)
For I am your provider and I meet all your needs (Matthew 6:31-33)
My plan for your future has always been filled with hope (Jeremiah 29:11)
Because I love you with an everlasting love (Jeremiah 31:3)
My thoughts toward you are countless as the sand on the seashore (Psalms 139:17-18)

And I rejoice over you with singing (Zephaniah 3:17)
I will never stop doing good to you (Jeremiah 32:40)
For you are my treasured possession (Exodus 19:5)

I desire to establish you with all my heart and all my soul (Jeremiah 32:41)
And I want to show you great and marvelous things (Jeremiah 33:3)

If you seek me with all your heart, you will find me (Deuteronomy 4:29)
Delight in me and I will give you the desires of your heart (Psalm 37:4)
For it is I who gave you those desires (Philippians 2:13)
I am able to do more for you than you could possibly imagine (Ephesians 3:20)
For I am your greatest encourager (2 Thessalonians 2:16-17)

I am also the Father who comforts you in all your troubles (2 Corinthians 1:3-4)
When you are brokenhearted, I am close to you (Psalm 34:18)
As a shepherd carries a lamb, I have carried you close to my heart (Isaiah 40:11)
One day I will wipe away every tear from your eyes (Revelation 21:3-4)
And I'll take away all the pain you have suffered on this earth (Revelation 21:3-4)

Jesus died so that you and I could be reconciled (2 Corinthians 5:18-19)
His death was the ultimate expression of my love for you (1 John 4:10)
I gave up everything I loved that I might gain your love (Romans 8:31-32)
If you receive the gift of my son Jesus, you receive me (1 John 2:23)
And nothing will ever separate you from my love again (Romans 8:38-39)

Come home and I'll throw the biggest party heaven has ever seen (Luke 15:7)
I have always been Father, and will always be Father (Ephesians 3:14-15)
My question is, Will you be my child? (John 1:12-13)
I am waiting for you (Luke 15:11-32)

Love, Your Dad
Almighty God

Tori: This is BEAUTIFUL! God's love for me is far more intimate than any ungodly relationship. I *want* to be *His*!

Comment On This · Love This · Share with Friends

Cal: When I started high school, I thought it would be cool to "get around." In a short time, I had a string of meaningless sexual relationships. I quickly became known as an "easy guy," but there were plenty of girls with no standards, so I maintained my cool because I was always "wanted." Then I met a girl in geometry class that was awesome. She was beautiful. She was funny. She had amazing goals and could carry on great conversation. Naturally, I wanted to date her, but she wanted nothing to do with me. I can't blame her. I wasn't a man of integrity. Why would a woman of integrity consider me a good catch? As ironic as it may sound, I called myself a Christian—even though I wasn't living it out—and so I confided in my youth director. To this day I praise God that I did. Not because I got the girl. I never did. But my youth director took me under his wing and started going through *Every Young Man's Battle* with me.[4] In doing so, I discovered how poorly I had treated myself and those girls and my future wife. My eyes were opened to God's incredible love and purpose in saving sex for marriage, and I'm proud to say that I've been abstinent ever since. I can't change my past. But I can say that for the last three years I have waited. I'm so thankful for God's goodness.

Comment On This · Love This · Share with Friends

Pam: Cal, AWESOME! I always tell people that I'm not as concerned about the choices they made before hearing the truth as I am about the decisions they make afterwards. You heard the truth and you chose to strengthen your character and become a man of *integrity*. Way to be a role model!

Comment On This · Love This · Share with Friends

Pam: Too many students today are looking for glass slippers to fall off at prom and not really evaluating their date on what *matters*—their *character!*

Comment On This · Love This · Shares with Friends

Stephanie: I made a mistake when I was 14, which I deeply regret. But I have made a commitment to God, to myself and to my future spouse to remain sexually pure from now until I marry. My question is, can you be too picky in what you look for in the people you date?

Comment On This · Love This · Shares with Friends

Pam: First of all, *good for you* for recommitting yourself to purity. That is awesome, and I am proud of you. I know that you are feeling like you can't find someone special for your life right now, but you should *not* compromise your standards. Remember, if you play now, you will *pay* later. But, if you pay now—with some dateless nights and a few of your peers thinking that you are crazy—you can *play* later.

Please continue to pray. If you are in a relationship with God, He will lead you in a way that will protect you and bring you joy. And *know* that there are young men of character out there. I meet them every day!

Comment On This · Love This · Share with Friends

📝 **Note: Homework for Your Future Spouse!** Take some time to write down the 10 character qualities the person you marry must have. Here are some ideas: Honest, Respectful, Empathetic, Compassionate, Good Work Ethic, Faithful, Courageous.

Please don't stop at words. Words are easy. Describe the character quality and write out how you want to see that modeled in everyday life.

Then, write down the 10 character qualities you will *not tolerate* in the person you marry and who will be the parent of your future children. Here are some ideas: *Rude, Disrespectful, Dishonest, Proud, Selfish, Boastful, Easily Angered, Lazy, Inattentive.* What do the 10 descriptors you chose mean to you? Again, write out how your words translate into everyday living so that your character examples are concrete and easily identifiable in potential dates.

After these qualities have been written down, take time to study your list. Are these qualities part of your own character? *Remember*, you always "get what you are," so if you want these in your dates, you need to live them out yourself! Second, make sure you have these character qualities etched into your mind so that when you are with a "potential date," you can evaluate that person *clearly*, without emotion. This will create required criteria for your future spouse and, like a job interview, you can make sure that you *don't date* until you know the person meets the qualifications for the spouse role.

Chase: I am falling for my current girlfriend. She is the most compatible person that I've ever been with, and she is falling for me as well. The problem is, she isn't a virgin. She fell to temptation years ago and has remained sexually pure since then. I, on the other hand, have stood strong and will until my wedding day. This really bothers me. I think this girl might be marriage material. Is there a biblical problem with a virgin marrying a non-virgin? Should I stay in the relationship? I just don't know what to do in a relationship where one is pure and one isn't.

Comment On This · Love This · Shares with Friends

Pam: I am glad that you wrote. You are in a difficult position as you wade through your emotions and think through the emotional "letdown" from this girl's past.

From a biblical standpoint, there is *no Scripture* that would suggest that you shouldn't be together. Just as Scripture is clear in its call to be holy, it is also clear that God is merciful. If you study the prophet Hosea, he was actually asked by *God Himself* to marry a prostitute. Why? Because God wanted a living lesson to the people of Israel that no matter how many times they were unfaithful to Him, God would always love and be faithful to Israel. Certainly this shouldn't be taken as a guideline, but it is a beautiful picture of the unfailing love and forgiveness of God, and it is a model of how we should all love and forgive each other.

I cannot, however, tell you whether or not you should continue in this relationship. Only God knows the answer to that. I do know that we have all sinned and needed God's grace and forgiveness from others. Our sins simply look different. So, if she has repented—and "years ago" indicates a pretty good window of time that she has remained committed to sexual purity—she deserves forgiveness. Forgiving doesn't mean that you have to stay in the relationship, though. That can only be determined through close prayer and reading of the Word so that you can feel God leading in the situation. He will guide you. Simply listen.

It sounds like this girl feels badly about her past choices. That is something that she can't take back, but "years" of abstinence indicates that she has taken strides in her character. Considering that some people who have sex continue to sleep around and think it "no longer matters" because their virginity is gone, she should be *proud* of herself that she chose better. She does care about her integrity, and she does care about her future husband, whoever he may be. That is honorable.

Pray together and keep communicating! I wish you *both* the best!

Comment On This · Love This · Share with Friends

💔 Jonah's Story

 When I was 13, I was in a dating relationship. Looking back, I can see what a poor choice that was. I shouldn't have been dating anyone before I could solve a simple algebra equation! My girlfriend and I were alone a lot. She lived next door, and our parents didn't get home until a couple of hours after school. Initially, we were innocent, playing basketball and doing our homework. But shortly after letting each other into our homes to do homework, we also started letting each other onto our couches . . . and not to do homework. I felt awful.

I secretly hated her for having sex, because it made me feel so bad inside. Three weeks later, we broke up.

Although I was young, I knew the devastation that came from premarital sex. I decided that I would *never* again have sex or foreplay until I was married. Immediately afterwards, that decision made a huge difference in my self-confidence and relationship with God. And I gained so much power and dignity in saying no.

The decision changed my life. I didn't date until late into high school. And I sat every date down on the first night and said, "My rule is no skin-to-skin and no alone time. I'll get myself into trouble and I don't want that for either of us." Some girls walked away, and that was fine. I knew they were the wrong people to be with.

Today I am engaged. I praise God for the healing that has taken place in my heart over the last eight years, and I anxiously anticipate my wedding day, which is just two months away. My desire would be that people know that God can restore what we break!

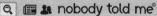

 Pam: Opposites might attract when it comes to *personality*, but they *never* attract when it comes to *character!* You will *get* what you *are!* Spend time working on who you are on the inside!

Comment On This · Love This · Shares with Friends

Chapter 8

The NEW Revolution: Romance Without Regrets

Pam: For those of you who are waiting—working hard at keeping your body, mind and soul pure—GOOD FOR YOU! Please know that you are *not* alone! You are *not* the last virgin on the planet! Purity is *worth it! You are worth it!*

Comment On This · Love This · Shares with Friends

Murielle: After hearing your message, I've decided to remain abstinent until marriage. I have been called a prude because I wouldn't have sex or engage in sexual activity, so thank you for encouraging me to keep my commitment!

Comment On This · Love This · Share with Friends

Trevor: My church shows your message every year. Two years ago, at the age of 16, I almost lost sight of how important my virginity was. My girlfriend really wanted to have sex, and she ended up breaking up with me over the deal. I was upset, but I'm proud of myself for remaining a virgin. I've seen how premarital sex tears relationships up and families apart, and I don't want to end up like that. Needless to say, every year, when I see your tape, I am reminded that I am not a loser.

Comment On This · Love This · Share with Friends

Rachel: I'm a virgin. And now, because of you, I am proud of it. For a while now, I've felt suffocated by the pressures about sex that today's culture shoves on us. I'm a Christian, and I believe that sex before marriage isn't right, but with all the stuff that I see on television and in the media, my beliefs had sort of . . . worn thin. The truth is, I started to think of my virginity as extra baggage wearing me down. Today I don't feel like that. *I'm* the one that has something special. Thank you for helping me to see that.

Comment On This · Love This · Share with Friends

Ciera: THANK YOU! I am a virgin, and I want to remain one until marriage. For a while I struggled with the whole "should I wait for sex until marriage or would 'love' be enough?" But, sex is a

huge deal. Thank you for inspiring me and reminding me how *great* virginity is. You probably saved my life.
Comment On This · Love This · Share with Friends

 Bethany: I can honestly say that I am a 100 percent virgin, and when I heard you speak, I was screaming "YES!" on the inside.
Comment On This · Love This · Share with Friends

 Pam: You are all awe-inspiring! Thank you for speaking up! Although society is telling you that you are animals, and that it isn't possible to control your hormones, you have proven them wrong! You are *human beings* with a *choice,* and you have had the personal integrity to make the *best choice*, not only for you and your future, but for those around you as well!
Comment On This · Love This · Share with Friends

📰 **Newsflash:** Fewer than half of all high school students report having had sex.[1] This means there are more students *not having sex* than those that are!

 Nathan: I would like to speak a word of encouragement to all young girls out there. When my girlfriend and I (I plan to marry her one day) began courting, she asked me point-blank if I was a virgin. Her reaction when I said, "Yes, I most certainly am!" touched my heart so deeply. Certain that she would never find a virgin husband, she *cried*. That made me realize how many other discouraged young ladies there are out there, and I will now go on the record saying that I joyfully waited and continue to keep myself for the woman that God has chosen for me. The best part is, I know for a fact that I am not alone. Don't give up out of desperation, because I am very grateful that neither I nor my future spouse did. I pray this reaches someone in her (or his) time of need.
Comment On This · Love This · Shares with Friends

 Pam: Thanks for your note! It will definitely inspire young men to stand proud that they have made healthy choices and will also encourage young women to trust that there are men of character out there. You are absolutely right. In today's high schools and colleges there are *many* young men choosing God's best. I get the opportunity to meet them every day, and I'm so proud when people such as you speak up about the respect they have shown to those they date.

You and your future wife will *never* regret following God's plan. Because you are building a godly foundation in your relationship now, you can celebrate all the gifts He has given for marriage in the future!
Comment On This · Love This · Share with Friends

Newsflash: Those of you who are abstaining will have the *best* sex. In one report, 72 percent of married traditionalists (couples who strongly believe that sex outside of marriage is wrong) report high levels of sexual satisfaction.[2] This is *higher* than *any* other group.

Brenna: You talk about a girl demanding respect from a guy and how girls should maintain an attitude that the guy is lucky to spend time with her. I'm new to the dating world, and I want to do it right. What do you mean by that?

Comment On This · Love This · Shares with Friends

Pam: Let me put it in this context. Some girls think that just because a boy has paid for the date (dinner, movie, and so on), she somehow "owes" him something physical. For example, girls have said, "He doesn't have very much money, and he spent what he had on me, so I should probably 'put out' if he wants me to." To me, that sounds like "paying for sex," or in simpler terms, "prostitution."

If a girl thinks like that, she should pay her own way. And if she feels pressured, she should *not be dating* that boy. The correct thinking is, "I am special, and he had the privilege of being with me." A girl does not *owe* a guy *anything* at the end just because he paid. Being with her *is* the reward. Make sure, however, that you are clear with *every* date *before* you ever go on that first date what your boundaries are so that there is *no confusion*. If you make it clear from the beginning, then no one is spending a date expecting something they will not be getting in the end, and it won't take long for you to find out the *true character* of the person you're dating. Most importantly, if they try to "push the boundary," it's *game over!*

As you enter the dating world, think this through *carefully*. If you don't think that you would feel comfortable standing your ground, *wait to date!* You have made a commitment to abstinence, so you need to be honest with yourself about when you are *truly ready* to date to protect your purity.

Comment On This · Love This · Share with Friends

Note: Strategies for Healthy Dating. Track is one of my favorite events in the summer Olympics. Filled with speed and excitement, track athletes soar over hurdles and challenge one another to become better in a race against the time clock. To the casual observer, their sport looks easy. They lace up their shoes and run in a circle. But the truth is that these athletes spend *hours* each day practicing.

For these athletes to succeed, they need to know how to time the course. If distance runners start in an all-out sprint, they will lose steam and falter at the end of the race. If the short track runners don't start right, they will immediately fall behind. Timing is everything, and if they are not *prepared* beforehand, a single mistake will cost them a successful finish.

The same is true in your Christian dating life. Paul wrote, "Do you not know that in a race all the runners run, but only one gets the prize? Run in such a way as to get the prize" (1 Corinthians 9:24). You *cannot* show up unprepared and expect to emerge victorious. If you want to arrive at the finish line (your *wedding* day) and win the prize (incredible sex with no past, pain or heartache), you have *got* to be prepared.

How do you prepare? Here are 10 training exercises you must conquer *before* you put on your shoes for *any* date.

- **Be absolutely convinced and fully aware of the consequences** if you fail to limit your sexual partner to one mutually monogamous relationship for life. Sex is a choice. You can say yes or you can say no. If you are not so confident in your no that you would *instinctively* run the other way once boundaries were pushed, you *need* to wait to date.

- **Write out your decision about sex.** Put a reminder of this decision someplace where you will see it and remember this commitment you've made to yourself and your future.

- **Develop self-esteem—believe in yourself!** If you realize that you are a person of worth, you will develop confidence. You *will not allow* a date to disrespect you, because you *believe* God when He says that your body is a temple of the Holy Spirit (see 1 Corinthians 6:19), and *never* would you want that defiled. You will *want* to "honor God with your body" (1 Corinthians 6:20) because your actions flow out of your thinking and your thinking will be grounded in the Word of God.

- **Practice assertiveness.** Everyone has the right to make decisions concerning his or her own body, especially when one's health is at stake. Practice giving a clear NO! Protect your *mind* by focusing on what is pure and right (see Philippians 4:8) so that you can more readily recognize and flee from sexual sin. In doing so, you will train your body to control its urges!

- **Communicate your boundaries to your date.** *Before* you even go on date number one you should have a discussion stating in *black and white* what your physical boundary is. There should be *no confusion* for either of you. If that discussion sounds uncomfortable or awkward, *cancel the date!* When boundaries aren't clear, couples find themselves in tears, saying, "Well, one thing led to another, and it was hard to stop." If you are mature enough to date, you need to be mature enough for this conversation. And don't end the conversation there. Make sure you talk together frequently about these important issues so that you can both work to *honor* each other's purity and make whatever adjustments are necessary along the way to stay away from places/positions of temptation.

- **Don't date individuals who are disrespectful of you and your boundaries.** This must be *cemented* in your brain, because Satan is a great deceiver. The lies will look *good*. So if you let your emotions get to you ("She's the most popular girl in school and she wants to be with me, so I don't want to run now"; "He says he loves me, so maybe it's okay"), you will be doomed for *failure*. You have got to focus on the *truth* and be strong *on your own* before you ever begin a dating relationship, so that if you get pressured, you can step back and reevaluate the relationship.

- **Plan your dates.** *Commit* to packing your dates with fun and positive things to help you get to know each other better. Too much time with nothing planned can get you into trouble. Again, if you feel uncomfortable telling your date that you want a plan to protect *your* integrity, stay home and wait until you are mature enough for this conversation.

- **Keep the Five-Minute Rule.** *Vow* that you will limit the amount of free time with no plans, because that *screams* opportunity for excessive physical contact. Limiting free time will prevent frustration and regret. You need to *feel okay* telling your date, "I've had a great time, but I would appreciate a ride home now, and we can plan something for another day."

- **Avoid alcohol and drugs!** Alcohol and drugs deaden the mind and the ability to think and make decisions clearly. You could come away from your "good time" with a great deal more than you bargained for!

- **Find a good friend with the same resolve to remain sexually pure.** *Prior* to dating make sure that you have an accountability partner. Ask a good friend that you are comfortable sharing with. This person should be able to grill you after every date to help you through pressure times and readjust your thinking should you get off track. Through this commitment, you will come away with a strong, valuable relationship—the makings of an amazing bridesmaid or groomsman!

 Brady: I've never before thought of "preparing" to date, but it makes sense. If I'm not spiritually equipped before I'm with someone I like, I will probably lose focus. Thanks for the practical steps!
Comment On This · Love This · Share with Friends

 Tiffany: It seems like my friends and I date just because it is the "next thing to do." Not because it is necessarily right. You have helped me to realize that mentality will harm me if I'm not careful. Being unprepared to date will lead to immature decisions that I will have to live with. It's time to start "training" so that I can look at my husband and say "I do" without regret. Until then, no dating for me!
Comment On This · Love This · Share with Friends

Pam: Good job! People who are able to stand strong and abstain until marriage are successful because they *work on themselves* first. When you get to your wedding day, I know that you will look back and be thankful that you *prepared yourself* and had *high standards* for your relationships!

Comment On This · Love This · Share with Friends

 Casey: I'm wondering if it's normal or healthy to pray for your future spouse. I don't even know who this girl is and yet I find myself thinking about her often.

Comment On This · Love This · Shares with Friends

 Pam: Praying over your future spouse is *crucial* to having a healthy relationship. As you pray, it will keep your focus on the *one* who is most important here, JESUS! This should reinforce your resolve to abstain and also help you to execute wisdom in choosing whom you will date. *Keep* praying and listening to God's voice!

Comment On This · Love This · Share with Friends

 Pam: Relationships are most fulfilled when we follow the advice "not to awaken love until the time is right" (Song of Solomon 8:4, *NLT*).

Comment On This · Love This · Shares with Friends

 Jackie: I love that Scripture. And I pray that God can use my story to empower today's young men and women.

More than 12 years ago, when I was 16 years old, I was like many teenage girls—interested in boys and being in a relationship. There was a guy that I met at work, Chris, who was super cute, and he asked me out! Of course I said yes.

We went to the movies on our first date, and he kept putting his hand on my upper thigh. I was confused because my other relationships were pretty pure, so I politely moved his hand, thinking he'd understand that I wasn't interested in moving so fast, and he'd be cool with it. He didn't quite get my subtle hint, and as the relationship progressed, he only seemed interested in going to parking lots and making out. He asked me to do physical things I didn't know about! I'd say no, but he was persistent, and I'd give in because I didn't want to lose him. I liked having him as my boyfriend.

As soon as I got my license, he asked me to come over to his house because his parents were out of town. I suggested we do other things, but he was only interested in my coming over. Five minutes after showing me the house, he said, "Let's go back upstairs." I was too shy to say no, so I followed. We started making out on the bed, taking off clothes. Then he said, "I'm ready to have sex." I quickly responded, "I'm not." Immediately, he said, "I want to break up." Shocked, heartbroken and confused, I said, "Five minutes ago you said you loved me, and now you want to break up?" He looked at me so cold in the eyes and said, "I said I loved you because that's what you want to hear."

Chris and I broke up (it was a two-month relationship). The next day, I went to school and heard you speak! I realized that if I had given in to Chris, he still would have broken up with me. I was so relieved that I made the right choice. I heard you a night or two later at a local church and was sweetly convicted that I needed God in my life. I was a Christian but not living for Him. It took another relationship and breakup to get me to hit rock bottom and finally sold-out to God! And I haven't been the same since!

Twelve years later, I have been married seven years to the man who waited for me and I for him. He is a youth pastor, and we talk openly with teens about sex and purity. Jake and I even waited to kiss at the altar on our wedding day (we dated for 6 months and were engaged for a year)!

I want to *thank you* for helping me. You have impacted my life and the lives of so many others.

Comment On This · Love This · Share with Friends

 Pam: God is *good!* His hand was on your life even when you didn't know it!

Comment On This · Love This · Share with Friends

💬 He Said . . . Charlie's Story

 "One day."

That seemed to be all I could think of while growing up. It will happen one day. It will happen when I am married. But will I get married, and when? Will I get to have "it"?

In the world of a high school boy or college boy, "it" seems to be all anyone can talk about, and you just wonder when "it" will happen. "It" is everywhere. Friends talk about "it." Movies and television throw "it" in your face. And all the while you just wonder, when will I get to do "it"?

If you haven't figured it out yet, "it" is sexual intercourse. And it is something that I remember as being the single greatest achievement in a young man's life. Now that may be a bit of an exaggeration, but it isn't too far off from how many boys think of sex.

Growing up, I was always told that "it" was something only to be shared between a married man and woman—that it is a big deal and is certainly worth waiting for. Basically, I was told that it would happen "one day."

Well, I made it through high school (nothing happened) and then it was on to college. I'd been dating Melissa since my junior year, and nothing like that had happened and wasn't going to until we were married. Not everyone shared that belief, however. Even my first roommate didn't wait for "it" and had a child while in high school to show for it. That was the first sign to me that there are consequences to your actions, even at a young age. So, as the years passed, I found out more about everyone else's sexual escapades in college and was definitely on the outside looking in when it came to sex talk in the dorms.

Now, it seems like this is all bad, but it isn't. I still had the same great girlfriend, and we were still waiting. As we became more serious, I constantly got more questions about it. "Why haven't you done it yet?" "Why does it matter that you wait until you get married?" "Aren't you going to get married anyhow? Just do it now." All these questions were out there, and they seemed very logical, to be quite honest with you.

However, I remembered what I was taught when I was young—that it is a very special action that is shared between married couples. Waiting is hard, but waiting is worth it. The reason you wait is so that on your wedding night you can look your soul mate in the eyes and know that you are about to experience something that neither of you have experienced before. The gift of sex is truly from God. He wanted us to enjoy it. And He wanted to make sure that when we did enjoy it, it was for the right reasons. Not just to satisfy a group of guys looking for a juicy story.

In the end, I discovered that it is great, and it is definitely worth waiting for. When you stop thinking about what you are missing out on and start focusing on what you can do to improve your relationship with your partner, your wedding night truly is magical.

💕 She Said . . . Melissa's Story

It was my junior year of high school. On the first day of Ad Room, he showed up as "the new kid," and I asked if he knew how to get to his classes. Sitting in our assigned seats next to one another, morning after morning, I discovered that there was a lot to this brown-eyed adorable cutie. He loved innocent fun. He loved his family. And he was deeply in love with the Lord.

Very quickly Charlie folded into my group of friends. We chatted on the phone often about the ups and downs of our day. And he started coming to the same youth group as me. About eight months after meeting, he asked me to "officially" be his girlfriend.

My response to him was this: "I will under two conditions. First, if a dating relationship doesn't work, your friendship matters to me, and I want to make sure you promise that we will still be friends. And, second, you can't be jealous about my close friend-ship with other guys." I would do a relationship with him, but not an untrustworthy, controlling, pseudo-marriage. He was okay with my conditions.

Although we were technically a "couple," we spent most of our weekends with our larger group of friends in both high school and college. Being alone didn't seem im-portant in our relationship.

In Charlie, I saw two characteristics I always knew I wanted in my future spouse. First, he was a man of faith. Even at 16, he wanted to go to church, and we could easily talk about our faith and pray with each other. And, second, he treated his fam-ily well. He honored his parents and wished he could protect his sister. He desired to spend time with them, gave them hugs and said, "I love you" to them often. In him, I saw a great husband and father.

A month after we graduated from college, I married my best friend. On our wedding night, we exchanged the letters we'd written to our future spouse and then enjoyed God's amazing gift.

To this day, I'm thankful for how we dated. Sex is powerful, but it can't sustain a cou-ple. There has to be "more." In him, I have more. After nine years of marriage, I con-tinue to discover that I love him more every day. He is a magnificent husband and a tremendous father; and those "highs and lows" we shared in conversations on the phone when we were dating, well, we still talk like that every evening, keeping us con-nected on everything impactful in our lives.

Pam: It is going to be hard, and you *will* get laughed at. But if anyone ever gets in your face, simply say this, "Any day, *tonight*, I could choose to be like you. But you will *never* again be like me." Once you have given your virginity to someone, it's gone!

Comment On This · Love This · Shares with Friends

Marissa: I'm 15 and a virgin. I've never been on a date, held hands, kissed or anything. I used to think that was a little weird because I looked at the rest of the kids in my class and how they acted.

Recently, I went on a 24-hour retreat to meet some people that I would be working with this summer. When we went to our cabin that night, the girls suggested we stay up all night talking. There were five of us, and we all climbed up on a few beds and starting chatting. Quickly, it became ev-ident that I was the only Christian there. And, apparently, "talking" meant talking about everything we've "done" with boys.

I sat back in shock while they all talked about everything they had done and continue to do, which involves a lot of sex and getting drunk. The girls wanted everyone to say how far they've been so we'd be more "com-fortable." When they got to me, I simply said, "not very far." Surprised, one girl asked if I'd kissed anyone, and when I said no, they all looked

kind of guilty. Then one girl said, "I wish I was still like that." To my aston-
ishment, they *all* agreed with her. I felt *so proud!*

Comment On This · Love This · Shares with Friends

Pam: What an encouraging story! *Never* be ashamed to speak
the truth. You will positively impact others through your decision
to abstain!

Comment On This · Love This · Share with Friends

Brittney: What if the people around you just don't get it? I chose abstinence early on and am fortunate to have a boyfriend who respects that.
But the people around me don't. They seem to think the only thing to do
is "mess around," and it makes me feel uncomfortable. Sometimes they
tease me and call me the "inexperienced virgin." It hurts, and it's so frus-
trating to feel like I am the one making the right choice and yet I'm the one
being belittled!

Comment On This · Love This · Shares with Friends

Pam: First, hear this: You *are* making the right choice. Words hurt
and your pain is real, but it is *nothing* compared to the pain of unplanned pregnancy, STDs, infertility or emotional heartache.
These peers are living in the *moment*. They are not thinking beyond "right now," and so even if they truly believe that it is cool and
it is fun and it is without consequence, they will find out soon
enough that they were wrong. You *cannot* walk outside of God's
protection and experience the promise, hope and fulfillment that
come through abiding in Him.

Herein lies the difference. They are getting their self-confidence
from who they are to others. *Who cares?!* At the end of time, they
are not going to stand before all of their high school peers. They
will stand before GOD! You, on the other hand, find your identity
through Christ and live in such a way that you can hear, "Well
done, good and faithful servant" (Matthew 25:21). I'd *much* rather
be in your shoes!

I'm reminded of James 1:2-4, which says, "Consider it pure joy,
my brothers, whenever you face trials of many kinds, because
you know that the testing of your faith develops perseverance.
Perseverance must finish its work so that you may be mature and
complete, not lacking anything." While tests are never fun, these
moments are defining your character. Will you sit with your lips
zipped, sulking in a corner, or will you speak out in love? You have
the *opportunity* to be a light, to stand up and explain why you are

making the choices that you are. Do not back down. If you do, you are selling yourself short, and your peers too! Consider this, what you say might just change their lives.

Comment On This · Love This · Share with Friends

💕 Ambrosia's Story

Last year I was in a very serious relationship. We were s-o-o-o-o-o "in love." He was my first boyfriend, and let's just say that I was far from his first. He wasn't a virgin, but he respected the fact that I was not going to have sex. Although he did respect my choice, it caused a lot of tension in our relationship. He just didn't understand why it was that I wouldn't give it up. It caused plenty of fights and we broke up last summer.

It's been really hard to get over it. And there have been many times when I've been tempted to give in just because in my mind that was why I lost the relationship. When you came to my school, you reminded me of all the reasons why I chose to stand my ground and got give in, no matter how hard it was.

Here's the amazing thing though. My ex-boyfriend and I had barely spoken since we broke up eight months earlier. After your presentation, he came up to me in the hallway and said, "Hey, I get it now." It felt *incredible!*

📝 **Note: Pledge to Your Future Spouse.** Having a physical reminder of your decision to abstain from this day forward will cement the commitment that you have made to God, to yourself and to your future spouse. While some students opt for a ring or necklace, others prefer private reminders. It doesn't matter what your visible reminder is *as long as you have one.*

We've created the following pledge for you. Relationships are a two-way street, and you need to make sure that you are choosing *integrity* to *guard* your body and *honor* your spouse. Please read through it, pray over it, sign it and then put it in your sock drawer, next to your toothpaste or anywhere that ensures you will see it and be reminded *every day.*

God's law was designed in love. We pray that you will submit to your Creator who loves you beyond measure and wants nothing more than for you to have a relationship beyond your wildest dreams.

My Commitment to My Heavenly Father, to Myself and to My Future Spouse

I recognize that in today's world the pressure to have sex is great. However, because of the physical risks, including pregnancy, disease, infertility and death, I won't give in.

I recognize that in today's culture the perception is that you can date just because and give your heart and body to multiple people without repercussion. However, because of the tremendous emotional risks, I will not give in.

I recognize that in today's society, people laugh off what God has to say and assume that His Word is outdated. However, because His Word is true and meant to protect me, I will not give in.

I recognize that I play a role in any relationship that I am a part of and that I need to be respectful of both my own body and those of people that I date because we are all created by Him and He calls our bodies temples.

I recognize that maturity in relationships is vital for true happiness both now and in the future. I will aim to always make decisions based on my core values, formed by God's Word and call on my life, and live in a right relationship with Him.

And so, I, _____, make a commitment on this day, _____, to abstain from all impurity of mind, body and heart until my wedding day.

 Pam: We are now seeing strong young men and women rise up from this generation who are speaking truth with words and with their lives to a world that needs to hear it. Will you join the NEW SEXUAL REVOLUTION? BE A REBEL!!

Comment On This · Love This · Shares with Friends

Endnotes

Chapter One: God's Amazing Blueprint

1. Christopher West, *Theology of the Body for Beginners* (West Chester, PA: Ascension Press, 2004), pp. 3-4.
2. David Hajduk, *God's Plan for You: Love, Marriage and Sex (The Theology of the Body for Young People)* (Boston, MA: Pauline Books and Media, 2006), p. 146.
3. Judy Lickona and Tom Lickona, "How to Tell Your Children the Truth About Sex," Catholic culture.org. http://www.catholicculture.org/culture/library/view.cfm?id=550&FID=32615381 &CFTO KEN=35723241 (accessed August 27, 2010).
4. John Eldredge, *The Ransomed Heart: A Collection of Devotional Readings* (Nashville, TN: Thomas Nelson, 2005), p. 49
5. Mike Mason, *The Mystery of Marriage* (Colorado Springs, CO: Multnomah Books, 2005).

Chapter Two: Unmasking the Lie

1. Several recent stories include the following: " 'Sexting' Leading to Criminal Charges for Teens," CBS News, January 15, 2009, http://cbs4denver.com/national/sexting. teens.crime.2.909154.html; Rachel A. Hutzel, "Mason 'Sexting' Students Sentenced," May 11, 2009, http://www.co.warren. oh.us/pros ecutor/community/press/2009/051109 students.pdf; Rita Braver, "Targeting Teens for Sexting," CBS News, May 31, 2009, http://www.cbsnews.com/stories/2009/05/31/sunday/main 5051909.shtml.
2. The National Campaign to Prevent Teen Pregnancy, "Sex and Tech: Results from a Survey of Teens and Young Adults," http://www.thenationalcampaign.org/sextech/ PDF/SexTech _Summary.pdf.
3. Clean Cut Media, "Teens: Imitating 87 Hours of Watching Porn," April 20, 2009. http://www.clean cutmedia.com/articles/teens-imitating-87-hours-of-watching-porn.
4. Rebecca Grace, "Porn-torn Home Called to Holiness," American Family Association Journal, October 2006. http://www.afajournal.org/2006/october/1006crosse.asp.
5. University of Iowa Children's Hospital, "Taking Control . . . Guidelines for TV and Teens," June 30, 2008. http://www.uihealthcare.com/topics/medicaldepartments/pediatrics/tvteens/ index.html.
6. Kate Klonick, "New Message to Models: Eat!" ABC News, September 15, 2006. http://abcnews. go.com/Entertainment/story?id=2450069&page=1.
7. Center for Disease Control and Prevention, "Healthy Weight—It's Not a Diet, It's a Lifestyle!" http://www.cdc.gov/healthyweight/assessing/bmi/adult_bmi/index.html.

Chapter Three: The Lies Get Personal

1. "Peer Pressure," The Free Dictionary, http://www.thefreedictionary.com/peer+pressure.
2. Domestic Violence and Sexual Assault Coalition, "Date Rape: The Importance of Consent," 2007. http://www.dvsac.org/resources/date-rape.cfm.
3. Office of the District Attorney 18th Judicial District, State of Kansas, Sedgwick County, "Teen Dangers," 2006. http://www.sedgwickcounty.org/da/teen_dangers.html.
4. Domestic Violence and Sexual Assault Coalition, "Date Rape The Importance of Consent," http://www.dvsac.org/resources/date-rape.cfm.
5. Rape Abuse and Incest National Network, "Statistics," 2007 data. http://www.rainn.org/ statistics.

Chapter Four: Math Meets Sex Ed

1. Elizabeth Terry-Humen, MPP, Jennifer Manlove, PhD, Hannah Brückner, PhD, et al., "14 and Younger: The Sexual Behavior of Young Adolescents," The National Campaign to Prevent Teen Pregnancy (Washington, DC: The National Campaign to Prevent Teen Pregnancy, May 2003). http://www.thenationalcampaign.org/resources/pdf/pubs/14summary.pdf.
2. Physicians for Life.org, "Study Linking Poor Pre-Abortion Counseling and PTSD Shows Need for New Legislation: Research Finds Poor Counseling Predicts Post-Abortion Psychological Problems," 2010. http://www.physiciansforlife.org/content/view/1845/26/.

3. © Mary Cate Bratcher, "An Uplifting Story About Love and Marriage," Renew America. http://www.re newamerica.com/columns/abbott/100111. Used by permission.

4. Rebecca A. Maynard, ed., "Kids Having Kids: A Special Report on the Costs of Adolescent Child-bearing," 1996. http://www.eric.ed.gov:80/ERICWebPortal/search/detailmini.jsp?_nfpb= true&_& ERICExtSearch_SearchValue_0=ED409389&ERICExtSearch_SearchType_0=no&accno=ED40 9389.

5. The National Campaign to Prevent Teen Pregnancy, "Preventing Teen Pregnancy: Why it Matters," Washington, DC: The National Campaign to Prevent Teen Pregnancy, 1996. http://www.thenation alcampaign.org/why-it-matters/default.aspx.

6. U.S. Department of Health and Human Services Administration for Children and Families, "Program Descriptions," 2010. http://www.acf.hhs.gov/opa/fact_sheets/cse_factsheet.html.

7. M. J. Brein and R. J. Willis, "Costs and Consequences for Fathers," in *Kids Having Kids: Economic and Social Consequences of Teen Pregnancy,* R. Maynard, ed. (Washington, DC: The Urban Institute Press, 1997), pp. 95-143.

8. P. L. Benson and A. Sharma, "Adopted Teenagers," *Adoptive Families,* vol. 2 (July/August 1994), p. 18.

Chapter Five: STDs

1. STD Information and Treatment Guidelines, "Sexually Transmitted Diseases Guide," 2005. http://std-gov.org/.

2. "Is Sex Safe? A Look at Sexually Transmitted Diseases (STDs)" (Boise, ID: Grapevine Publications, 2001).

3. Melissa R Cox, ed., *Questions Kids Ask About Sex: Honest Answers for Every Age* (Grand Rapids, MI: Revell, 2005), p. 135.

4. Teens4PureEnergy, "Sexual Exposure Chart," http://www.teens4pureenergy.com/teens4/ chart.htm.

5. The Medical Institute for Sexual Health, "What Makes Adolescent Females So Susceptible to STIs." http://www.medinstitute.org/public/125.cfm.

6. J. R. Cates, N. L. Herndon, S. L. Schulz and J. E. Darroch, "Our Voices, Our Lives, Our Futures: Youth and Sexually Transmitted Diseases" (Chapel Hill, NC: University of North Carolina at Chapel Hill School of Journalism and Mass Communication, 2004).

7. "Sexual Development and Health: Condoms," 4parents.gov, 2005. http://www.4parents.gov/top ics/contraception.htm.

8. Amy Oliver and Diana Dukhanova, "Depo-Provera: Old Concerns, New Risks," Different Takes, Hampshire College, Spring 2005, no. 32. ttp://www.global-sisterhood-network.org/content/view/ 218/59/.

9. "Hormonal Birth Control and HIV AIDS," http://www.epigee.org/hiv_birth_control.html.

10. The Medical Institute for Sexual Health, "How Many STIs Are There and What Are Their Names?" http://www.medinstitute.org/public/121.cfm.

11. Center for Disease Control and Prevention, "Chlamydia—CDC Fact Sheet: How Common Is Chlamydia?" 2010. http://www.cdc.gov/std/Chlamydia/STDFact-Chlamydia.htm#Common.

12. Ibid., "Chlamydia—CDC Fact Sheet: What Complications Can Result from Untreated Chlamydia?" http://www.cdc.gov/std/Chlamydia/STDFact-Chlamydia.htm#complications.

13. Miriam Grossman, MD, *Unprotected: A Campus Psychiatrist Reveals How Political Correctness in Her Profession Endangers Every Student* (New York: Penguin Group, 2007), pp. 111-112.

14. M. Y. Hwang, "The Silent Disease," *Journal of the American Medical Association,* 1998, vol. 280, no. 6, p. 582.

15. Center for Disease Control and Prevention, "Gonorrhea—CDC Fact Sheet: How Common Is Gonorrhea?" http://www.cdc.gov/std/Gonorrhea/STDFact-gonorrhea.htm#common.

16. Ibid., "Gonorrhea—CDC Fact Sheet: What Are the Complications of Gonorrhea?" http:// www.cdc. gov/std/gonorrhea/stdfact-gonorrhea.htm#complications.

17. "Drug Resistant Gonorrhea on the Rise," MSNBC, 2010. http://www.msnbc.msn.com/ id/18076491/ ns/health-sexual_health/.

18. Ibid.

19. STD Information and Treatment Guidelines, "Sexually Transmitted Diseases Guide," 2005. http://std-gov.org/.

20. The Henry Kaiser Family Foundation, "HIV/AIDS Policy Fact Sheet," March 2008. http://www.kff. org/hivaids/upload/3029-08.pdf.

21. Albany University, "Abstinence, Condoms, and Safe Sex: Sorting Out the Confusion," 1994. http://www.albany.edu/sph/AIDS/abstinence.html.

22. The Henry Kaiser Family Foundation, "HIV/AIDS Policy Fact Sheet," March 2008. http://www.kff. org/hivaids/upload/3029-08.pdf.

23. Center for Disease Control and Prevention, "Genital HPV Infection—CDC Fact Sheet: How Common Are HPV and Related Diseases?" http://www.cdc.gov/std/HPV/STDFact-HPV. htm#common.

24. Center for Disease Control and Prevention, "Genital HPV Infection—CDC Fact Sheet: How Common Are HPV and Related Diseases?" http://www.cdc.gov/std/HPV/STDFact-HPV. htm#common.

25. Sean Alfano, "FDA Approves Cervical Cancer Vaccine," CBS News, June 8, 2006. http:// www.cbs news.com/stories/2006/06/08/health/webmd/main1696099.shtml.

26. National Cancer Institute, "Human Papillomaviruses and Cancer: Questions and Answers," February 14, 2008, http://www.cancer.gov/cancertopics/factsheet/Risk/HPV; Centers for Disease Control and Prevention, "What Is HPV?" http://www.cdc.gov/hpv/WhatIsHPV.html.

27. U.S. Food and Drug Administration, "FDA Approves New Indication for Gardasil to Prevent Genital Warts in Men and Boys," October 16, 2009. http://www.fda.gov/NewsEvents/News room/Press Announcements/ucm187003.htm.

28. Sean Alfano, "FDA Approves Cervical Cancer Vaccine," CBS News. http://www.cbsnews.com/sto ries/2006/06/08/health/webmd/main1696099.shtml.

29. U.S. Food and Drug Administration, "Gardasil Vaccine Safety: Information from the FDA and CDC on the Safety of Gardasil Vaccine," August 20, 2009. http://www.fda.gov/Biologics BloodVaccines/ SafetyAvailability/VaccineSafety/ucm179549.htm.

30. CDC National Prevention Information Network, "Genital Herpes/HSV." http://www.cdcnpin.org/ scripts/std/std.asp#1d.

31. Elizabeth Boskey, PhD, "Living with Herpes," About.com, August 2, 2010. http://std.about.com/u/ua/her pes/herpesuserstories.htm.

32. Medical Institute for Sexual Health, "Genital Herpes—Get Your Facts Straight." http://www.med institute.org/public/98.cfm.

33. Physicians for Life, "General STD Info: Everything You Really Don't Want to Know." http://www.phys iciansforlife.org/content/view/206/37/.

Chapter Six: When Chemistry Is More than a Subject

1. J. D. Teachman, J. Thomas and K. Paasch, "Legal Status and the Stability of Co-residential Unions," Demography, November 1991, pp. 571-583.

2. Joe S. McIlhaney, MD, and Freda McKissic, MD, Hooked: New Science on How Casual Sex Is Affecting Our Children (Chicago: Northfield Publishing, 2008), pp. 39-40.

3. Marcia Segelstein, "The Science of Sex," Perspectives, June 16, 2009. http://www.onenews now.com/Perspectives/Default.aspx?id=567964.

4. McIlhaney and McKissic, Hooked: New Science on How Casual Sex Is Affecting Our Children, pp. 39-40.

5. Eric J. Keroack, M.D., FACOG and Dr. John R. Diggs Jr., M.D., "Bonding Imperative," A Special Report from the Abstinence Medical Council.

6. McIlhaney and McKissic, Hooked: New Science on How Casual Sex Is Affecting Our Children, pp. 41-42.

7. Bill Albert, "America's Adults and Teens Sound Off About Teen Pregnancy: An Annual Survey" (Washington, DC: National Campaign to Prevent Teen Pregnancy, 2007).

8. Joan R. Kahn and Kathryn A. London, "Premarital Sex and the Risk of Divorce," *Journal of Marriage and the Family,* November 1991, pp. 845-855.

9. Rebecca Hagelin, "Sex, Sadness and Suicide," The Heritage Foundation, June 3, 2003. http://www.heritage.org/Research/Commentary/2003/06/Sex-sadness-and-suicide.

10. Denise D. Hallfors, PhD, Martha W. Waller, PhD, Daniel Bauer, PhD, et al., "Which Comes First in Adolescence—Sex and Drugs or Depression?" *American Journal of Preventive Medicine,* October 2005, vol. 29, no. 3, p. 169.

Chapter Seven: Repentance and Renewal

1. "Crisis Pregnancy Centers," http://www.choicesaz.org/sexual_health/sex/index.shtml#secondary_virginity.

2. Barbara Wilson, *Kiss Me Again, Restoring Lost Intimacy in Marriage* (Colorado Springs, CO: Multnomah Books, 2009), pp. 108-109.

3. Father's Love Letter, http://www.fathersloveletter.com/text.html.

4. Stephen Arterburn, Fred Stoeker and Mike Yorkey, *Every Young Man's Battle: Strategies for Victory in the Real World of Sexual Temptation* (Colorado Springs, CO: WaterBrook Press, 2002).

Chapter Eight: The NEW Revolution

1. Center for Disease Control, "Youth Risk Behavior Surveillance—United States, 2009," *Morbidity and Mortality Weekly Report,* June 4, 2010, vol. 59, no. SS-5. http://www.cdc.gov/mmwr/pdf/ss/ss5905.pdf.

2. Joe S. McIlhaney, MD, "Is Premarital Sex Worth It," The Medical Institute for Health. http://www.marriageromance.com/stories/10802697703.htm.

About the Authors

Pam Stenzel for years was on the "front lines" as director of Alpha Women's Center, a counseling center for women undergoing crisis pregnancies. Her experiences taught her that before teen pregnancy and STD rates could decline, attitudes of teens toward sex first had to change. Desiring to bring about that change, Pam started speaking nationally full-time. Today, she is in great demand both in the United States and in other countries such as Mexico, Canada, Australia, Ireland and South Africa. Drawing from her personal story, as well as her visits with teens around the world, Pam talks about the consequences—both physical and emotional—of sex outside of marriage. It's been her experience that today's young people, if given the facts, are fully capable of making good, healthy decisions.

To book Pam for your conference or your community, go to **www.pamstenzel.com** and click on "**Bring Pam**." To order DVDs and curriculum for both church and public schools, go to **shoppamstenzel.com**. If you have a question or story you want to share with Pam, go to **www.pamstenzel.com** and click on "**Ask Pam**."

Follow Pam on twitter.com/Pam_Stenzel
Facebook Page: "Fans of Pam Stenzel, Speaker and Author"

Melissa Nesdahl, after seeing the effects of pre-marital sex on her peers, began educating area teens at a crisis pregnancy center about the physical, emotional, and spiritual risks of sex outside of marriage and the benefits she experienced firsthand in choosing abstinence until marriage. Melissa recognized that when students understood who they were in Christ, they chose the best for their body and future. Combining her passion to write with her love of sharing truth, Melissa routinely updates her website, writes product and curriculum with Pam Stenzel, is a monthly contributor for MODSquad (Mothers of Daughters), and shares other writing projects and articles.

Follow Melissa on twitter.com/#!/MelissaNesdahl
Website: www.melissanesdahl.blogspot.com

Join the *Nobody Told Me* fan page on Facebook and give us your feedback! We would love to hear from you!!!